It's our universe, Red.
Everyone else just lives in it.
Love always.
Your T

Derailed
Inwood Indiana Press
www.InwoodIndiana.com
Mishawaka, IN

Design and editing by Glenn Lyvers.
Printed in the U.S.A.
Inwood Indiana Issue 3

Derailed

Contents

Turns

Rochester Charlie is a panel away
coughing up a lung in his slum across the hall,
no different than my own, and I am struck
by the idea that he will never have sex again,
and that I think might be crying in-between the
darkness and the divider. He is pitiable but unwelcome
and even the dog glares at the thin wall, wanting nothing
more than to be left to the quiet darkness, to sleep
on this side of the panel that separates us from him.

I do not know if he will die tonight, or if the sun will
shine on his face again. Tonight, he has only the moon,
framed in the window, raping the sun's brilliance,
shining absurdly in the night sky, a ridiculous pretender.

I imagine someone should be notified, or maybe
someone should help him get clean. An angel
must walk the streets, some caring soul who might
stumble upon him in the sunshine, and smell his presence.
One who sees through his matted hair and notices the
protrusion of his ribs. I know angels exist; there are
women who reach out with clean hands, pale hands,
hands that can save a man.

I do not know if Rochester will die tonight, or if the world
will turn into tomorrow, arresting the imposturous moon,
revealing the sun or an angel for him—perhaps the last
one, leaving nothing for me.

Glenn Lyvers

Immobile

The truck rolled slowly and perilously up the icy hill. Dark trees, miles of snow and the endless night sky panned and dipped slowly across the vehicle's windows as it plodded upward. Eliot Moon refused to expose his fear to his father, and feigned nonchalance as he caressed the steering wheel, but it took all he had to rein it in with even the slightest bump or swerve. His knuckles were as white as the evening snow.

"Positively gothic," judged Dr. Moon from the passenger's seat. He was most likely referring to the looming convent in the foreground, a structure built by pious innocents a century ago, which now resembled something a lazy teamster might've painted onto the backdrop of a 1950's B horror movie: all steeples and archways, missing only the token bolts of lightning overhead. There would be no lightning tonight to disrupt the cold stillness of most other nights that this region had to offer come winter.

Dr. Moon had been surprisingly quiet up until now, which was itself a small blessing. Perhaps the sight of the convent in this dark wilderness, which lacked subtlety in a way that probably offended him, triggered his gruff. "The flu," he mumbled to himself. "An entire convent gets the flu. These women live in the Dark Ages. Deluded old virgins, forgotten by time."
Eliot said nothing, because deep down he feared nuns. He never met one, so the fear was irrational. But the idea of nuns terrified him. Dr. Moon despised all churches and religious figureheads, but had occasionally admitted to a grudging respect for the ladies of the cloth. They generally lived simple, healthy, long lives, which in his medical book spoke great volumes. That is why he agreed

to respond to this late call, an act of great rarity on his part. He admired the nuns' lifestyle, not their calling.

The truck nearly sputtered a sigh of relief after it was parked into a small lot behind the convent, which looked much smaller up close than it did from the bottom of that high hill. Eliot opened the door for his father, who leapt spryly onto the snowy tar of the lot. The older man belonged on the cover of a baby boomer magazine: he was fit and strong, his bald head and knife-sharp silver beard only accentuating a potent masculine prowess. Eliot passed the leather black medical bag to his father and began to follow him around to the front door, but halfway Dr. Moon spun to face him.
"You're not going in there," he told him. "This abominable place is a holy Petri dish of contagions. I will not have you loafing about the house, whining and spreading around your foul smoker's phlegm, and missing more work. Start warming the car in twenty minutes, and don't you dare smoke any of those damn cigarettes that I'm supposed to pretend I don't know you have."

Eliot watched as his father leapt up the icy steps to the front door with abandon. Was there a surface on earth strong enough to crack the old man's skull if he fell? Was it even possible that he could fall?

Convinced that he was finally out of Dr. Moon's line of vision, Eliot lit a cigarette. He had made his way slightly downhill and off the path, now finding himself in the dark, cold, silent forest. Eliot spent his days crunching tree trunks into particle board at the mill, and tall trees in the wilderness often made him feel guilty, threatened and unarmed. But better to smoke beneath these evil trees than in sight of his father, whose venomous medical sermons cut him deeper than any saw.

As he puffed on the little burning knob, the usual thoughts crawled lazily through Eliot's mind. He wished the mill would go union; a rumor had spread that a guy at the union mill several towns over had "accidentally" severed the tip of his finger on the head saw and was given a lifetime of disability payouts.
He wished he could be back in New York City, in Greenwich Village with bohemian Aunt Peggy, where he spent the happiest fourteen months of his young life while his mother was sick so many years ago. The memory of those lights and colors, songs and smells; those happy drunk college students and their sidewalk bric-a-brac, were now fading into half-recalled dreams.

He wished that he didn't have the face of a horse and the voice of a dormouse, so that he could get the nerve to spark up a conversation with the check-out girl at the Mobil Station off of Exit 21, who was the only pretty girl Eliot had ever seen within twenty miles in any direction. He wished he could be anywhere else and anyone else but Here and Him.
The first scream was so muffled and quick that Eliot just assumed he hadn't heard it. It couldn't be a scream; it was an afterthought. He smoked on.

The next one came long seconds later. It was a bleating, inhuman wail, undeniable in its awful eeriness. It came from no direction, and had no discernable proximity. It dropped a hard chill onto Eliot, who froze in place, mind and body.
The third scream brought more purpose and less mystery. Perhaps it was just Eliot adjusting to this new stimulus, but he could now read more from it. A woman, deep in the woods, beneath the hill, away from the convent. A woman in pain.
A woman being raped. Murdered. Mauled.

The cigarette butt fell to the ground. Eliot heard his heavy breathing and felt his heart thump wildly in his ribs. He was making a crunchy mess of the snow beneath him as he began running in one direction, stopping, backtracking, beginning in a new direction, stopping, backtracking, etc. Where should he go and what should he do? The convent. His father. Cell phone. Police.

The fourth scream pulled him blindly into the dark woods below him like an invisible claw. He had to act. He had to stop this. Where was he going? His brain clattered within his skull like a coin in a shaken bucket. What would he do? The dark trees whipped around him as he leapt down over roots and branches, stumbling, slipping, but not falling. What was he prepared to see? His mind floated above his body, but the body soldiered downward, following the fifth scream.
The trees cleared and Eliot stopped running, and was now sliding down an icy hill, on the soles of his boots, like he was roller-skating. Here was a cemetery. A fucking cemetery, beneath the ledge he had landed on. A sixth scream rose from below him, and Eliot was so scared that he almost began to cry. Then he looked down.

In the deep snow bank beneath his icy-rocky perch, some yards from the gravestones, lay a large figure, seemingly making snow angels. It took a long moment for Eliot to summon back control of his organs to determine what he was seeing. It was a heavy woman, lying face down in the snow. She was not making snow angels, she was merely clawing feebly at the snow around her to try and regain leverage, but she was failing. She had fallen. And now she was screaming.

Eliot hated himself when he realized he was stifling a laugh. Perhaps it was out of relief that the big reveal had not proved more dire, and that he did not have to fight a bear or a murderer. Perhaps.

After a mercifully brief moment of pondering, Eliot slid down this slope with the same ease as the one above it. He began to silently marvel these stuntman athletics of his, triggered in a moment of chaos. Who knew?

Ankle-deep in the snow bank, Eliot jogged to where the large woman lay.

"I'm here," he announced breathlessly as he approached, "I'm here."

The woman began to cry when she heard this, but could not angle her head to view her savior. Eliot stooped low to meet her gaze. Her dark eyes were pink and puffy, and her round, childish face was deathly pale. Her mouth was agape with sobs.

"What happened?" Eliot asked.

The woman was trying to formulate words between her blubbery bleats.

"I fell," was all she could legibly muster. She repeated this several times.

Eliot reached for her wide hands, which were spread out before her.

"No!" screamed the woman pathetically. "You can't get me up by yourself! I'm too big! Get help!"

On a normal night, these words would've moved him to pity and embarrassed obedience, but tonight Eliot was feeling cocky. So he took a firm grip of her wrists and began to pull her up. She was heavy, but the adrenaline that pumped through his body made Eliot into a human forklift. Soon the woman was slumped over his shoulders, and then standing before him more or less on her own, but she was wobbly and continued to tightly clutch his hands. She proceeded to shake and sob.

"I was trying to take a shortcut to the path over there," she finally warbled after regaining an inch of composure, motioning with her head to a small footpath going up a

side of the hill leading up to the road that, sure enough, would've made Eliot's downward journey a lot more practical. "I don't know why I walked here. The snow is so deep. I don't know what I was thinking."
Eliot furrowed his brow in puzzlement. "It's not so deep," he replied.
The woman burst into new tears, and now Eliot finally felt the good-old fashioned guilt reclaim his body, stifling the adrenaline rush down with a forceful wallop. He had said the wrong thing.
"Let's go," he told her, and began to release one of her hands, but she held on for dear life.
"I can't, I'll fall again," she whimpered.
"Okay," he answered, "Okay. Let do this."
Hands locked with hers, Eliot began to pivot the pair of them in a circular fashion towards the path, side-stepping. She followed his lead in this strange little dance. When they finally reached the relative safety of the path, the woman cried out in relief and hugged Eliot tightly.
"You saved me," she whispered. "You saved me, you saved me." A strange warmth basked over Eliot as she cooed this into his ear.

The slow march back up to the convent proved relatively quiet as the woman began to regain her composure. By the time they had been let in by one of sisters, pale and unresponsive in her illness, she gone quite silent. Perched on a bench in the waiting room, the woman silently gasped, eyes closed, exhausted. Her entire body was damp from the snow and the sweat. The simple cotton muumuu she wore clung moistly to her folds, and her surprisingly bare legs dripped small rivers through her fleshy crevices. The rolls of her leg fat draped over her ankles, nearly hiding her slippers.

The older nun who let them in lingered only briefly before retiring to her chambers, too sick to stand there and tend to them. Eliot caught glimpses of other nunly figures spiriting down hallways in flickering movement, younger ones pushing older ones in wheelchairs with remarkable speed.

Dr. Moon had been summoned, and was now questioning the woman as he tapped her brow with a cloth and pulled a thermometer from her mouth. He was trying out his best bedside manner with her, but even this was fraught with chilly sarcasm.

"Well, you are very lucky to have escaped diphtheria, Virginia," he told her, calling her the single name she had given him earlier when pressed. His reeked of adult condescension, and clearly Virginia immediately knew what she was up against and hated him.

"Your son saved me life," she replied simply. Dr. Moon merely took a mental note of the mercury in the thermometer before returning it to his bag.

The youngest and healthiest nun in the convent, a silent woman in her fifties, was now swaddling Virginia's bare legs with paper towels, mummifying them. It was grotesque and sad for Eliot to behold, but his father's lack of response to Virginia's declaration made it seem all the more depressing.

"And what brought you to the cemetery at this hour?" the doctor finally continued with half-interest. Perhaps his father could get some sort of punchline out of this line of questioning, Eliot pondered.

"I realized I had forgotten to put flowers on a grave," she answered curtly.

"Ah, I see, I see," Dr. Moon added with a dramatic nod. "A lost lover, perhaps? Husband?"

"My mother's. I'm not married."

"Of course." Dr. Moon then balked as if he caught

himself in an outward display of obvious cruelty. This was not his style, at least not with anyone other than Eliot.
"And where do you live?" he proceeded, switching gears.
"Half a mile down the road, off Exit 19."
"Well, that's quite a walk for you."
Virginia flashed him a cold stare. "I took a taxi."
Dr. Moon nodded again. "I see, I see. Well, you live, for now. But, Miss Virginia, I must warn you that a person of your immobility must really consider some serious lifestyle changes before deciding to go on a late-night gallivant through a cemetery snowdrift."
"Dad," Eliot heard himself interjecting. The nun had stopped her swaddling and looked up at the doctor coldly. Dr. Moon quickly turned back to his son, sporting a stoney frown, but Virginia held up a hand, nodding patiently.
"It's okay, Eliot," she announced sadly, "It's fine. I've had this conversation a thousand times with a thousand men just like this one. And I'm tired of discussing my glands, my diet, and everything about my body. It's pointless, and it's not worth it. So, I'll just call a cab and be on my way. Thank you again, so much, Eliot."

Without once looking back at the woman, Dr. Moon leaned in to whisper to his son. "Take her home, and come right back. Don't listen to a thing she tells you. Just drop her off and get right back here. I'm tired of this nonsense, and these people."

Despite her ordeal, Virginia now smiled sweetly from the passenger's seat of truck where she was precariously squeezed into. She was murdering the vehicle's suspension and the truck nearly scraped the tar, but Eliot did not mind so much. He was transfixed by the sudden change of mood from his passenger as the convent dropped out of sight behind them.

"How did you find me?" she asked, staring at him with her warm chocolate eyes and her sunny round face, framed under strawberry bangs.
"I was out there smoking," Eliot responded sheepishly. What's going on here, he wondered.
"Thank God for that," Virginia said with a gentle laugh. "Thank God you smoke."

Eliot awoke from a strange, pleasant dream with a cruel chemical jolt, darting upward from the couch where he normally slept. Dr. Moon hovered by him, fully dressed for a day at the office, shaking his resigned head. He was absently stuffing the remnants of the smelling salts back into his pockets.
"Go to work," he commanded before quickly exiting the house.

The day had passed languidly, and Eliot was surprised to get through it uninjured, given the state he was in. His thoughts had been darting awkwardly between wanting to know why Virginia had seemed so at ease with things last night in the truck, and what the inside of her house looked like. And he had never seen eyes so wide or a smile so kind. And no one had ever called him a hero before.

"These are for a friend," Eliot heard himself telling the checkout girl in the Mobil station. "She's going through a rough time. These should cheer her up, right?" This had been the most he ever said to the checkout girl. Or to any girl, more or less.
"Sure," she replied, not even looking up at him. "That'll be eleven fifty."

"The kettle doesn't whistle anymore," Virginia called from the kitchen, "But I always know when it's ready.
Eliot fidgeted on the puffy couch adorned with an Afghan rug. His gas station bouquet spread modestly from a jar,

newly perched on the little coffee table before him. The house was a descent size, but dilapidated. Many chachkies adorned shelves and surfaces, depicting animals at play or rest. The woman emerged with two blue mugs and their flapping tea bag strings hanging from them, and sat down on the loveseat across from him.

"No one's brought me flowers in a real long time," she said with quiet sincerity after a pause.

The worst thing about blushing is the tingling heat one feels in their cheeks.

"I dunno if their considered nice or not," he babbled, "it's not my thing."

"They're nice," she assured him with a smile. "And if if you didn't bring them, it's so nice that you came to check up on me. You're just nice, I guess."

Eliot nervously sipped the tea. "This is good."

"Yes. You bought it for me, sort of. Welfare, I mean. It's from the taxpayers."

Eliot looked up at her.

"I have to be honest," she continued gravely. "I'm not proud of it. I have three undergraduate degrees: Library science, computer science, English. But no one wants to hire me. And I don't know if I could get to a workplace if they did."

Eliot didn't quite know what to say, so he said the first thing that came to mind. "Never did college."

She eyed him curiously. "How old are you again?"

"Twenty-two."

Another kind smile. "And you can't guess my age. No one can. I like it that way. It's one of the perks of being like this."

She was correct, but Eliot could never guess anyone's age. He wasn't good at that sort thing.

"You should give college a thought," she continued. I mean, you're father's a doctor. You can afford a great school. I had to do the community college. And even that wiped me out."

This was not a conversation he wanted to have. "Not for me."

She searched his soul with a warm, penetrating gaze, then suddenly shivered, and clung her large sweater tighter around her shoulders.

"It's cold in here," she said. "That air conditioner over there is rusted into the wall. I threw a blanket over it, but that didn't do much. I hope these flowers make it through the week."

The flowers lasted about three days, but they remained wilted in the jar when Eliot returned. On the fourth week, it was Eliot himself who decided the brown rotted things must be tossed.

He did not care much for the opinion of others, regarding who saw him with Virginia or who did not. Not like there was much to worry about if he did: Virginia always preferred his visits at her place. The home she inherited was cluttered, but she kept it neat enough, and it always felt inviting and safe compared to Dr. Moon's stark little house.

Eliot did not fully understand his attraction to Virginia. She was certainly not the physical type he had become familiar with in women, and by all means was raised to resent anyone who "did not take care" of themselves physically. But truthfully, Virginia actually led a pretty healthy life. She ate well, exercised to the best of her ability, and was hygienic. But she was born with problematic glands, and there was nothing she could do about that. He admired her acceptance of this, and appreciated how devastating a setback like the night in the cemetery could be.

He had to admit that Virginia's constant reminders of his heroic acts that night, as well as her regular reassurance of his attractiveness, intelligence and overall goodness, had become a bit of a drug. He caught himself becoming less embarrassed with her compliments over time, and this revelation nerved and thrilled him.

Aside from this ego boost, conversations with her were also intoxicating. She listened well, and she spoke of interesting things, like places she'd like to travel to and jobs she'd like to have in those places. Eliot began to see himself in other places around the world, away from this nowhere town, for the first time. Perhaps he and Virginia could leave this place behind and get their fresh starts somewhere else entirely.

The only person he went out of his way to hide his friendship with Virginia from was his father, of course. It wasn't so much that Dr. Moon had any sort of power over him per se, but the man had a way of producing such a vicious turn of phrase. Eliot did not think he could listen to the awful things the hateful doctor had to say about Virginia.

It was on the day that Eliot was finally able to wrestle that damn rusted air conditioner out of the hole in Virginia's wall that life became even more interesting. It started with her hand on his shoulder, which turned into a caress of his arm.

All the things that Dr. Moon had to say about fat women were wrong. Everything about her body was soft, warm and inviting. He fell into her, and with every inching movement there was another part of her to explore. She roared with delight. It was wonderful.

Love consumed him, for the first time. There was no point in calling it anything else. Virginia opened up even more after this first lovemaking; she became more real, more human. Her encouragement and praise never stopped, but he found that she had begun to gently prod him into a forward movement. Where could they take this? What should they leave behind? What did they need to do to make this into an actual life together?

"I heard about you and your friend," Dr. Moon told Eliot one day as the younger man was rushing out. Eliot froze and eyed his father, who stood with his back to him, gazing out the window, a cold little marble statue. Such a small figure, casting such a large shadow.

"What's that, now?" Eliot asked, knowing full well where this was going.

"A doctor friend of mine told me all about it. I'm surprised that behemoth of yours still manages to come in for check-ups. She went on and on to him about her new young lover. I obviously knew right away. I was repulsed, but I knew that only you could ever be so stupid as to– I can't even say it. I can't even imagine it."

Eliot hung his head, ashamed of his shame. "I didn't think you doctors were aloud to talk about that stuff," was all he could say.

"No one but fools live here, in this town. If that weren't the case, I'd warn you against the social improprieties of being seen with such a person.

Eliot flashed with angry heat. He just wanted to get out of this house, forever and ever.

"Well, if that's the case, then you really don't have much to complain about, Dad. I'm just another fool."

The doctor turned around. Eliot was expecting those beady little death orbs burrowing hatred into his chest, but was instead surprised to see that Dr. Moon's eyes were opaque pools of sadness.

"You don't remember your mother's illness all that well," he began. "I sent you away at the worst of it and I don't regret it. The meningitis twisted her spine into a an abstract thing, and she screamed herself to unconsciousness, and I was right there screaming along with her. And then she screamed herself to death, and I was left wondering whether or not our twenty years of relative happiness together was worth it for me, to have to see her in those final moments."
A lump formed in Eliot's throat, and he was rendered mute. He had only the vaguest, most idealized memories of his mother, but the image of her as a screaming, knotted pretzel was too much for him to process. He had never really been told this before.

"Falling in love with a sick person is the height of folly," Dr. Moon continued gravely, sad eyes lost in thought. "You will be left alone, questioning the point of everything, and you will grow into a cold person."
Eliot recovered as quickly as possible. "Virginia isn't sick. She's just gotta different shape, is all. She's healthy enough."
Dr. Moon shook the languidness from his expression and frowned familiarly. "And what does she want to do with her life, this Virginia? What are the great plans you two have for the future?"
"I dunno. We'll work something out."
"I am sure you're convinced she's self-sufficient, but I am going to go out on a limb and suggest that she's on assisted living, is that correct?"
"Just for now, but she's gonna get a job soon."
"She will get no job," Dr. Moon growled emphatically. "She will continue to blame the world for her problems, and she will suck the resources out of everything and everyone around her. She will leave you a dry husk, and you will be stuck in this town you hate so much forever

and ever."
Eliot felt dizzy, and slumped onto the couch. Nausea crept its way up into the pit of his stomach.
Perhaps, for a fleeting moment, something resembling pity could be traced in his father's expression. Eliot remembered the first and last time he saw this look, years ago, as the doctor faded from view while the train carried young Eliot to New York City.

But the moment was indeed fleeting, and the gears turned again in the doctor's presentation.
"Do as you must. I don't own you. I did a rotten job of raising you and there's no point in starting now.
"But you should know this. Your Aunt Peggy called a few weeks ago, and wondered if you had any interest in working as a superintendant in that maddening little building of hers in the East Village.'
Eliot shivered. This was too much.

"I wasn't sure what to tell her," the doctor continued. "You've been out of the house more than usual these past few months. I thought perhaps you were finally resigning yourself to life in the particle board business here, and that this rural idiocy was maybe your real calling.
"Tell me. Was I wrong in drawing that conclusion, Eliot?"

Eliot was frozen in the truck. Every exterior and interior square inch of the vehicle was packed with items, wrapped in paper and plastic and tied with bungee cords.

Virginia's house loomed in the passenger window, looking smaller and colder in the moonlight this evening then he had remembered. He hadn't spoken to Virginia in weeks, leaving her voicemails unanswered. Avoiding her proved alarmingly easy, despite the pleading, desperate confusion of her messages. Listening to Virginia's recorded raves and rambles as she tried to work out the reasons of his betrayal in monologue form infused Eliot with a detached coldness, like he were listening to an avant-garde radio play. He knew that his father's words had gotten to him: perhaps she really was a being of endless need and limitless blame. Perhaps she had been about to reveal these to be her true colors. Perhaps he was getting out alive while he could.

If that was the case, it did not explain why Eliot could never bring himself to actually explain to Virginia why he had her cut out, or that he had officially cut her out at all. It did not explain why the mere idea of saying goodbye to her would completely paralyze him.

He gave the little house one last look. Perhaps she had already forgotten him by now. Maybe she'd find the strength she needed to gain her mobility, and move on to better things. Or maybe she'd remain in that house, in this town, until the end of her days. Eliot hoped that wasn't case.

Realizing he was crying, Eliot drove off, accelerating more with each mile, praying for the moment to arrive when this frosty little town would drop out of the rear view mirror for the final time.

James R. Silvestri

Chemical Imbalance

It took me until 3AM to really figure out what the doc had told me earlier in the day. Of course, I had plenty of distractions. It was Tuesday evening, and we were in the usual rush to get Barton Weekly News ready for the printer Wednesday morning. As Editor-in-Chief, I had plenty to do.

"Merle! Are we going to print that Letter to the Editor from Darryl Thompson or not?" my wife Annie yelled at me across the room, as the bitter cold February began to creep in around the edges of our poorly insulated office. She looked much the same as she did seven years ago when we got married. Shoulder length, jet black hair framed her delicate face, and her gorgeous green eyes. Despite her genteel appearance, she was all business at the paper. Because we had been unable to have kids, this newspaper was her kid— the focus of all of her energy.

"Do the layout as if it's in," I mumbled back, "but I've got to read it again. It's such bullshit. I hate to publish it. But if we don't, all of Darryl's friends will write us next week and complain. Its only midnight; we've got plenty of time to decide. Ed, how you comin' along with your stories? We gonna be OK on them eh?"

"Yeah, should be good. 'Barn Fire' is just about done. Just gotta figure which picture to use; got some more to do on 'High School Wrestling', but shouldn't be too long," said Ed Bolton, the last of the reporters still in the office working on his copy. Ed, a good head taller than both Annie and me, with long, brown, curly hair, shifted his trademark toothpick into the gap between his top front teeth. "How's your back?"

"Its fine," I said, disregarding the pain that had begun to break through the Percocet the Doc had given me. "I can't imagine what it would be like for you to actually get something done on time."

But his question brought the whole cascade back to mind: a slip on the ice while fishing last week, landing on my back, persistent pain which took me to the Doc for the first time in a decade. The CT scan he ordered showed a small fracture, which explained my pain. But it also showed a surprise: a tumor in my right adrenal gland. Doc told me that my tumor was pumping large amounts of steroids into my bloodstream, and probably had been for years. Malignant or not, the tumor would have to come out.

"Gimme a break. For what you pay me, you're lucky I'm here at all." Ed's reply brought me back to the present.

"Only kiddin', Ed."

For that entire evening and night I was brooding on it. The headlines slowly came into focus. They were: 1) I have a tumor that has to come out. 2) I have been on steroids for a long time. 3) When the tumor comes out, I will be coming off of the steroids, and I have no clue how that will affect me. That evening, I mainly came to grips with the first headline, but I was quite optimistic I would be just fine. No problem. I would just deal with it.

"Done! Here you go, Sugar," Ed said as he gently, almost tenderly, pressed his thumb drive into the palm of Annie's hand and smiled at her. It struck me as an awkward maneuver for someone as rough as Ed.

"Thanks," Annie said as she looked away from him, flicked her hair back, and plugged the thumb drive into her laptop. "That about wraps it up. 2:30 AM. That's early for a change!"

"See you Thursday, Ed." I said as Annie and I closed up the office.

"Hope you feel better," Ed replied, as he pulled the hood on his parka up over his head, put on his gloves, and opened the door to the developing snowstorm outside in the bleak middle of the night.

<<<<>>>>

Next morning I was up at 8AM, instead of sleeping in as I usually did on Wednesday. Thursday starts next week's cycle, so Wednesday is my break.

Annie heard me rustling around in the kitchen, came out, poured some coffee, and sat down at the kitchen table.

"So what do you think about what Doc said?" Annie asked as the toast popped up. She brushed back her bangs and her green eyes squinted at me, a signal that she wanted a real answer.

"He told me that they'd remove my right adrenal gland, including the tumor. It's about the size of a golf ball. He says that's easy. Very successful. 99%. He does it through a laparoscope. No big incision. Home the next day. He says my other adrenal gland is normal. It'll take over. No big deal. I'll need to take steroids for a while after the operation, but that'll only be for about six weeks."

"Why the steroids after the operation?" Annie asked looking confused.

"Been used to high levels of steroids for a long time. Can't just go cold turkey. I'll need to be weaned off."

What she didn't ask was whether or not the tumor might explain our trouble with getting pregnant. I had actually asked the Doc that question, but his answer was a hedge. "Hard to say," Doc replied when I asked him, "Lots of possible factors for infertility; this could be one." I thought it was a dodge to a simple inquiry. I wished I had asked some follow-up questions to get more clarification. So I was glad Annie didn't corner me about it, because I didn't have an answer.

<<<<>>>>

I don't really remember too much about that day. I was ready. The Valium, or whatever they gave me before the surgery, made me feel like I was in love with everyone. After the operation, I remember waking up in my room and focusing in on Doc. He told me that everything went great. Annie was there, and I had very little pain. Life and the world seemed beautiful. If anything hurt, all I had to do was push a little button and I would get some morphine. I felt great, and happy to have the operation behind me. I would be able to go home the next day. Looking back, those few hours were probably the high point of my next decade.

<<<<>>>>

"Merle! What are you doin'?" Annie shouted at me as I got up to get a beer from the fridge. She had been home with me for the entire 48 hours since I came back from the hospital. So much time together in a small home in the middle of the winter in Vermont was starting to take its toll. Her normally fresh appearance was beginning to look a little worn around the edges.

"Getting' a beer. What's the problem?" I hadn't shaved for four days, which is far from normal for me; nor had I been out of the bathrobe I came home in. So I was looking and feeling a little scruffy myself.

"You know the problem. Doc told you to just hang out for a few days. You just had a big operation, but I can't keep you down. Why won't you just let me get you things for a couple of days?"

"I can't stand having you get me stuff. It doesn't seem natural. The tumor is out; everything went great; I feel good, and I think I can get myself a beer."

"Doc Phillips warned you that you would feel better than you really are—

especially early in your steroid wean. You've got to take it easy."

"It'll drive me crazy just sitting around," I countered. "Can't wait to get back to the paper."

"Merle Williams! You know very well what he said: at least six weeks before you go back to the office. Don't make me fight you on that," she said, rolling her eyes.

"So how will things work while I'm off?" I asked as I cracked open the Heinekens.

"It'll be fine. I'll fill in till you get back. I can do that and the layout work on Tuesday night to put it to bed. The other reporters will do what they have always done. I'll need some help to organize stuff, make assignments, set the schedule, make calls on advertisers . . . that kind of stuff. Ed can do that fine till you get back."

"Ed?" I said, jumping up. "Why Ed? He's just another reporter like all the rest. What makes him so special?"

Fact is that Ed, Annie, and I go back a long way. We all graduated from North Country High School ten years ago. He was the center on our regional championship basketball team, while I struggled as second-string guard. He was a tall basketball hero and I was a short, heavy set, square guy who rarely got into the game. He and Annie were an item most of the way through our senior year. But I was the editor of our high school newspaper. Ed never actually talked about the fact that Annie dumped him for me. It happened the autumn she and I went off to University of Vermont while Ed stayed at home doing odd jobs, and working on the family farm. Winning Annie was one of the high points of my life.

So I was surprised when, three years ago, he applied for a job as a reporter at my Barton Weekly News. Even though I really didn't like him, I felt I should hire him so I wouldn't look like I was holding a grudge. At the age of 25, I was young to be running a newspaper, even if it was a weekly in upstate Vermont. In fact, I was the youngest Editor-In-Chief in the paper's 55 year history. So I wanted to appear quite professional.

"Simple, Merle," she said as she vigorously flicked back her hair and squinted at me. "All the others are part-timers. They've got day jobs or don't want to do more than one story a week, or two at the most. Ed's different.

The News is his life. It's his big thing. He can organize people, make assignments, all of that stuff, so all I need to think about is putting it together and getting it to the publisher."

"OK. I see," I said, although it didn't seem right to me. I viewed Ed as a rube . . . a fool. I couldn't imagine him actually managing people. But I had no choice. At that point I was recovering from surgery and Annie was running things till I got back. I'd have to clean up the mess when I returned. I couldn't wait to get back in the driver's seat.

<<<<>>>>

It was six weeks after my operation, and time to get back to work. I was almost done with my steroid wean. Right after the surgery I couldn't wait to get started, but now that the time was here, I wasn't quite as excited. I really didn't have the energy I was used to. One reason may have been the 15 pounds I put on just sitting around for six weeks, on steroids, eating a lot, and not exercising at all. I didn't like looking at the extra chin I had developed as well as the jowls.

Winter had begun to break and we had drifted into mud season, that time in Vermont between the beautiful snow, ice, and crisp air of the winter, and the mint greens and fragrant blossoms of the spring. Between those two times of year is mud season: dreary, raw, wet, and brown. Nothing but mud on the roads, fields, porches, and rugs. Even in the best of times, mud season's no fun. If things aren't great, it's downright depressing. Plus I was home alone a lot. Annie was spending more and more time at the paper with Ed to get the work done. That was beginning to bother me.

I thought I would start off slowly by just showing up at the shop. A Thursday morning meeting would be good.

That's where we plan the next week's paper: decide on stories, assign people to cover them, review advertising income, and the various things that make a small weekly newspaper work. That way I could get a feel for what had happened over the time I have been gone.

Annie and I had discussed my re-entry. Since she was Editor-in-Chief in my absence, she was running all of the meetings. Ed Bolton had managed to slip into the second-in-command position despite my objections. Every time I would challenge Ed's apparent rise in power, Annie countered with endless examples of Ed's extra work. He had done way more than his share of the stories and Annie had even brought him along on the lay-out work. Of course that meant many late Tuesday night/early Wednesday stints to get it done. She actually mentioned to me once that Ed had made some advances toward her during one of those sessions, but she assured me she told him to knock it off. The rest of the crew were part time reporters who simply showed up to get their assignments at the meeting on Thursday, and handed in their story sometime Tuesday. The whole arrangement was worrisome to me and I wanted to get things back to normal as quickly as possible.

I found myself weirdly uncomfortable as I got ready to drive over to the paper that first Thursday morning. Her plan was for me just to just sit back and observe the first meeting, joining in as I felt comfortable. I reminded myself that I had run the paper for over a decade by myself with a little help from Annie. This should be no problem. Yet being away from it for six weeks, and having the paper be successfully run by my wife and her former beau, was a little unsettling. It felt like the first day jitters when I was a kid at the beginning of the school year.

"Hey Merle! Welcome back, guy!" Ed Bolton shouted out the moment I slipped in the room through the back door.

"I wanted you all to be surprised," said Annie. "Merle has bounced back quickly, and he talked the Doc into beginning to come back to the paper, at least part-time."
The other three chimed in their welcome backs, and after a little more banter, Annie resumed control of the meeting. She turned it over to Ed, who handed out the assignments, keeping the most important or interesting ones for himself.
Ed was looking at me funny. I figured that jerk was noting my extra weight or the beads of sweat on my forehead from just walking in from the car. I was really out of shape.
Just as I was mentally planning my exit, Ed blurted out "I've got a great idea for the big feature of the week: Exclusive interview with Merle Williams: Back from surgery and better than ever!" It sounded sarcastic to me.
"I don't know about that, Ed," I immediately replied. This was the first I had heard about that idea, and I hated it. I wasn't ready to go public with this whole chapter of my life. I was still processing a bunch of stuff, and I wasn't sure I knew how I felt. For sure, I didn't like the idea of that story being reported by Ed Bolton, of all people. If anybody, it should be Annie. Also, I was not feeling particularly buoyant. I had begun to wonder if I was becoming a different person than Annie married. What was happening? How much of the man that Annie married was the steroids, and how much was me? I was getting nervous about that question.
"Maybe we can do that in another month or two," Annie finally chimed in, mercifully. . . . a little early, yet," she said as her eyes meant mine. She had read my mind.
At home, that evening was probably my low point. On my favorite sports radio talk show, the caller was rehashing the controversy over Barry Bonds going into the record books with 71 home runs in 2001. Now, years later, it has become almost a certainty that he was on steroids at the

time. He was re-asking the question whether his record should have an asterisk after it . . . whether it should really count. His point was that it was the steroids, not the real Barry Bonds that accomplished the feat. I couldn't help but wonder if there will be an asterisk after my major accomplishments: winning Annie from Ed, and being the youngest head of the Barton Weekly News.

Four weeks after that first time back, Doc liberated me to go back to work full-time. Take it easy, he said, as if I had the energy to do anything else. I sure didn't feel like the same person I was before I lost my tumor. I felt bad. I was pessimistic about the paper and life in general. For a while, I even considered just staying on part-time and letting Annie continue to run the paper. But I couldn't stand her spending that much time with Ed. So I decided I needed to return full-time and take back my old job.

<<<<<>>>>>

Maybe it was just having made that decision, but later that week, I was feeling a little better as I sat on our porch overlooking the pond on a perfect spring evening after dinner. Mud season had finally yielded to spring, the air was mild, and the days were finally getting longer. I watched one of the most beautiful sunsets I have ever witnessed. The reflection of the sun had just met the sun itself on the water as it sank behind Hedgehog Mountain. The symphony of colors had commenced its parade of hues, finally settling on indigo as Annie joined me on the porch. She had been strangely quiet as we ate, and refused my help cleaning up in the kitchen. Something was wrong.

"Pretty sunset," I cast out into the evening air just to say something.

Several minutes later she broke the silence. "Yeah it is," she said as she shifted position in her Adirondack rocker. "I'm thinking about getting back to the paper next week. .

. .I'm feeling halfway decent, so I thought I would give it a shot" I announced. "We'll have to figure out what to do with Ed, now that I am back in action, and won't need him acting as some kind of a big shot."
"Ed has done a spectacular job while you were out," she said sharply. "You just can't blow him off by sending him back to his old job! I was actually going to give him a raise, and promote him to Managing Editor."
"He's only a reporter, nothing more. Moving him up won't add anything except an extra layer of management that we can't afford." I said mustering a diminishing amount of energy for the fight I saw brewing. "It's no time to add more salary expenses, given the stinking economy and everything that goes along with that."
By this time Annie was beginning to cry. Softly at first, and then more violently. "What happened to the guy I married? You were a kick-ass, get the job done, guy who never worried about a thing. Now you're doom and gloom. You used to be fun," she said as she slumped down in her chair. Instinctively, I went over to give her a hug. As I held her, she shook, and I tried to comfort her.
"Don't worry about it Annie. I'm sorry. Well figure it out. We don't need to decide anything tonight. We can talk about it tomorrow."
"Merle, I have something to tell you."
A long silence.
"What's that?"
"I'm pregnant."
The remaining indigo of the lingering sunset yielded to a roll of dark clouds on the western horizon which slowly, one by one, began erasing the stars.

Terry Davis

The Closet Legacy

Dana, the younger brother, had not seen the North Arlington house for so long the sight of it came up hard against his memory. It now seemed such a modest house from the outside and small inside, not much bigger than his condo– kitchen, living room, family room, bedrooms, the one bathroom– all smaller than he remembered or wandered through in dreams. The furniture seemed smaller too. The dark mahogany dresser, his father's, was no higher than his shoulders, his mother's companion piece was just waist high, and everything was within reach. He picked up a Lladro figurine, a dandy in a tri-corn hat, from his mother's dresser, then put it back down. He knew he could get something for it, but something told him to leave it alone. It was too soon for that, and he would do better to take in the bedroom, the whole house, as it had always been. His parents' twin beds, after all, were the same, as was his mother's writing desk against the window, and when he opened the blinds the view outside in the Saturday afternoon sun was the same—the backyard apricot tree, the long privet hedge screening the property next door, the small opening he could crawl through to escape his older brother, Victor.

Down the hall, their own bedroom was also the same. Their boyhood furniture was still there—another twin set, maple, a matching double dresser, two carrel desks, and their window view of the front yard, Wynn Lane and Dr. O'Brien's house across the street– shadier but about the same. The bedroom closet, though, was in disarray. Both folding doors were off their hinges and leaning against the wall. The inside was piled high with cartons marked "Documents," "Checks," "Photos," and a range of years from his father's boyhood to his own and Victor's, a jumble of dates and boxes stacked randomly. Of course, all their old things were long gone, their pressed clothes and good shoes–Victor's on the right until he left for college in California—and boyhood things they had shared from time to time—the stray hats, baseballs and board games on the shelves, the fishing tackle, racquets and bats leaning in the corners, things that had also led to fights.

He re-arranged two or three boxes of photographs and albums that seemed about to topple over, but he was not about to sit down on the edge of his old bed and start leafing through them. They included him, of course, but they still seemed more his father's property than his own. He focused more attention on the home movies—eight-millimeter reels in canisters stacked behind the shoeboxes, some of them as old as his father's childhood but most of them from his own and Victor's. There were dozens of canisters marked with titles on masking tape—Victor and Dana Swim Team, First Bicycles, Victor/Football, Dana/Halloween, Yellowstone/Grand Tetons, and Birthdays, Birthdays. The old projector in its case and a screen were there, and he recalled how the bar in the family room had been perfect for setting everything up, something he could do himself as a boy while the adults sipped their cocktails. Nowadays, he reflected, people did not watch their old home movies, but transferred them to DVDs– much easier to set up, if just as boring—if they watched them at all, after spending all that money. In any case, his father, likely to stay put in an assisted living complex, could hardly operate a newfangled DVD player any more than he could remember how to work an old movie projector.

He left the closet doors as they were and walked back to the kitchen for a look in the refrigerator. He found a single bottle of Irish beer behind a spoiled carton of milk.

As he fished in a drawer for a opener, he wondered why the movies ended up in their old closet, moved from the family room cabinets, handsome built-in cabinets on both sides of the fireplace, the obvious and better place to store them. Their mother had been dead for years, and surely their father had not been up to it. Only Victor could have moved them. Was Victor planning to take charge of the whole archive, estranged, unsentimental Victor? He got the top off and drank the beer over the sink. It then occurred to him the home movies were a unique part of the family archive. Unlike many of the old photos, the movies were an only copy of the past and should be preserved, however expensive it might be. As the older and by far wealthier, Victor should see to this, he told himself, and, lately, he did seem more civil– a change in tone Dana had noticed when they talked a week earlier about a bill from White Beech. The bill should have gone to Victor, not to himself, and Dana had phoned him at his home in McLean on a Sunday afternoon. Victor said he was surprised to hear from him and asked him how he was.

"I have a bill for two hundred dollars," Dana replied. In the background he could hear music, laughter, people in the swimming pool, Julie, Victor's wife, laughing, and he pictured Victor sitting on the terrace with a drink. "It's for a walker. Can you believe that? Two hundred dollars, some special kind of walker."

"Dana, it's what they go for and a used one at that."

"Well, you said in your letter you would be picking up the uncovered expenses."

"Don't worry about the bill. I'll take care of it. As it is, Dad can't use the thing much. He can barely get out of bed or the wheelchair now, not without someone to lift him. I could send it back, but he has some idea he might need it in case of fire. He thought there was a fire last night, and apparently rolled out of bed onto the floor, then tried to pull himself up. They found him stretched out by the walker with some cuts and bruises on his legs. We got him back in the bed, and the doc came by to bandage him up."

"Don't bother. I went ahead and paid the bill myself, and since I have you on the phone I think we should agree on who is going to start keeping up the house. It's a mess—full of dust, and the fridge should be cleaned out. Everything in it has spoiled, and one of the closets has both doors off. I think you know which one."

"Dana, I'm advertising for a tenant, and I've lined up a cleaning woman for two days a month. Again, don't worry about the money. Dad still gets ten percent of everything the law firm makes, not to mention income from two annuities and Social Security. I'm writing his checks and he has plenty of cash in a number of accounts, large amounts in CD's and a respectable fortune in Treasuries."

"Do you have a key to let her in?"

"The cleaning woman? She starts Thursday, but I'll have to let her in and out. He doesn't want anyone alone in the house, and I can't talk to him about it. He doesn't have the attention span. I have one key. He lost his. He can't remember where it is."

Dana did not want to press him about a key for himself. Victor, he knew, would not let him have a key, even though he might say he would. But, beyond Victor's usual possessiveness, he was not worried– He knew he could get in the house on his own whenever he wanted.

Today, he had used another key, the back door key, found where it had been hidden twenty years ago– in a sandwich bag under the birdbath by the apricot tree. When they were both in high school, he had looked out the kitchen window and seen Victor put this key in the bag, tilt the birdbath and hide it underneath. He did not blame Victor entirely for the subterfuge. Their father would not let the boys have house keys, not even when they were in their teens, and Victor in desperation had lifted a key from his mother's purse and taken it to Bede's Hardware for copying. Mother had found out, then father, and there was a row. Victor had thrown a punch at his father.

Dana finished the beer, saw the trash bin was too full to take anything more, and left the bottle on the counter. The matter of the key gave him some pause, and, as he thought more about it, he began to doubt Victor's civil tone. Perhaps there would be no point in calling him again and bringing up the home movies more explicitly. If he did, Victor might agree to take on the expense of saving the archive and then do nothing of the kind.

He walked out the back door and locked it. Looking at the birdbath, he realized he could not hold on to the prospect of a reformed, magnanimous Victor and put the key in his pocket. Why indeed had Victor moved the archive from the family room to their old bedroom closet and said nothing about it? What was he up to? The albums and the home movies– especially the home movies—might have offended him early on, and moving them around was perhaps some tactic in a strategy to get rid of them. Half the images were of the two boys together. Dana at least looked happy as a child, but Victor, he remembered, seemed resentful at every age, at every event. Perhaps he wanted the fleeting joy of possession only to throw everything away—a joy more satisfying than rcconciling around their father's deathbed.

True, Victor did see his father at White Beech and often, but that did not mean he liked the old man anymore than he liked his brother or had liked their mother. He probably disliked all his relations– Their very existence would have wronged him. His general demeanor had softened somewhat, but underneath must lurk the envious first child and the bully.

Someone, Dana concluded, had better save the archive from Victor, and when he reached his car door he knew he would have to do it himself. He would load up his car—perhaps this week—then drive home and up to the storage room door off the lower level of his building, and somehow make space in his bin. It would be a challenge, but at least the movies would be safe from Victor. Victor had been a difficult, resentful child. Everyone said so. If he did want to make amends by keeping up the house before selling it, so much the better. He could afford to do such things–He was now a partner in his father's law firm, and, after all, he was the older brother.

He said nothing further to Victor about the closet. That evening, however, he did bring the matter up with his wife, Erica Wong Watmaugh, his second wife. They had not been married long, but they had known each other for years as colleagues in the Department of Motor Vehicles interviewing people who had mislaid their licenses or needed their traffic citation records. She saw right away where he was going and cut him off—

"What are you thinking? We don't have any room here. We live in a condo not a house. The closets are too small as it is. The building is old, and the closets are small. All the rooms are small, and we don't even have a dining room. The bathroom is small. One bathroom, and it's small like the closets. The closets are jammed, and don't even think about the storage bin. It's a joke, slapstick joke. Stuff tumbles out like a joke when you open it up. Let Victor take those movies. He has plenty of room. He lives in a big house in a nice neighborhood with lawns."

"I'm not sure I trust Victor with the movies. It's like an archive, you know, a family archive."

"Victor and his wife even entertain people, rich people and lawyers from his divorce cases. I used to talk to Marty Vandever from traffic court, and he knows all about Victor's firm and his money. Victor makes more than your father did. I've been in your father's house two, three times, and if you want to take something out of that old house don't take some old movies. Take his bedroom furniture. It's no good to him anymore. He's never going back there. Get rid of the crummy bedroom furniture you bought for this crummy condo. Give it back to the curbside where the people pick up divorced man's kind of furniture. It's total crap, and we are married two years. Your parents' bedroom pieces are mahogany, good quality. You told me you had money and I should quit my job, becoming happy homemaker, but if you're not buying me a decent house at least provide some decent furniture. I'm not asking for whole house of furniture, just one bedroom set, no big deal."

She walked into the kitchen, and he waited before he followed her. She was taking a pound of hamburger out of the freezer.

"Well then, why don't you take all of Dad's furniture?" he said, "the living room, dining room pieces?"

She turned around and looked at him. "His living room is wicker, and the dining room table is glass with wrought iron chairs, like patio furniture. It looks odd, like it doesn't know where it belongs, inside or outside.

Bedroom set is fine, master bedroom– not the spare bedroom with that exercise stuff, and not your old bedroom furniture, kids' furniture, definitely not that. Master bedroom is still good. Victor is probably over there already with movers loading it up in a truck."

"I'm not sure I want my parents' bedroom set," he said, "not in my own bedroom. And I'll tell you about odd. It seems odd to me, familiar but at the same time odd, like I'm sleeping with them, an aura of them."

"What in hell are you talking about?"

"The furniture you want."

"I don't feel any aura."

"And it's a twin bed set, you know."

"I prefer twin beds, and let's not get into that."

She went back to the hamburger. He walked out of the kitchen, then outside into the building hall, then back in. She was chopping onions, and he stood in the kitchen doorway.

"All right," he said, "which parent's bed do you want for your bed?"

"It doesn't matter."

"It might matter to me."

"In that case I want your father's bed."

"Why my father's?"

"I said it doesn't matter to me."

"Is it because you want to sleep in my father's bed or because my mother died in her bed?"

"Grow up. Your father is seventy- two years old. It's furniture, just furniture. I'll use Kam Douglas, Cousin Nancy's boy, and he can use the pickup from their business, swimming pool service. A big kid, really big, and it will help her out too. She calls me on the phone yesterday and she says, 'My God that boy eats! He's eating me out of house and home! He's bringing his friend Cyril over for dinner last night, someone he's meeting at pool, and this is disturbing me.' So I tell her, I tell Nancy, 'Sounds like a nice rich boy with pool for your business.' And she says, 'No, not rich boy, and not nice but loser, dropout, tattoos all over. The kid is someone he's meeting at pool room in Manassas and not at swimming pool mansion.' "

"I don't want any kids like that in my father's house."

"We're both laughing hard on phone about this, about pool and pool, but she is then still going on about this Cyril, who is a bad influence on Kam Douglas. So I think we should use Kam Douglas, pay him a little extra money so he won't get involved with this guy in any shady kind of deals. Then at the same time she is telling me Cyril has his own truck and does odd jobs. So today I'm thinking we can use him after all to help Kam Douglas with moving furniture—nothing else, just moving–then bring the boy over here for dinner when he's done moving the furniture– not both boys, just Kam Douglas. I have turkey roast in the freezer– but don't let him bring Cyril. They can do it Sunday afternoon, only day of the week Kam Douglas can do it because of his job. Two trucks, and the two boys can do it in one trip, three hundred dollars. He can use the extra money, a nice boy compared to Cyril, but not long enough in this country. His English is poor, holding him back. And I'll have him take your crummy bedroom set to Salvation Army in Manassas, no extra charge. Better say two hundred dollars for each boy. You can afford that at least– a little extra to keep him away from Cyril and some shady deal, who knows what."

"I want him to bring a few other things from the house," Dana said. "And I want him to bring all the old home movies with him, plus the projector and the screen."

"All right, I give you that."

"They're in my old room in the closet. Have him put everything in the storage bin here, even if you have to take some things out to make room, things of yours I should think."

"Your father won't even know about his furniture. You won't have to bring it up with him. He's not even sure where he is most of the time."

When he thought about seeing father at White Beech, Dana might have said as much himself, but on his next visit, the staff physician, Dr. Flores, told him his father was improving. He was now on a drug regimen newly approved for geriatric care, apparently more aware of his surroundings, and he could stand up and take a few steps without falling. There was yet more encouragement from Dr. Flores–

"Mr. Victor Watmaugh, Senior can go back home, provided he has a caregiver for at least part of the day to clean him up and fix one hot meal."

Then a physician's qualifier—

"And no, I can't say how long the results will last. I see some patients on this regimen with dramatic improvement for as long as three, even six months or longer. They can move into the apartments, if they want, or go back home. It's still new, so we really don't know how long it could last."

That evening, Dana told Erica the good news.

"A part-time caregiver, that's all he needs, and it's less than we're paying at White Beech. The first thing we'll do is get him back home in his own bedroom with his own things. I need to line up the caregiver, someone who can cook. Still expensive, of course, but less than now."

She looked up from her TV Guide, frowned, and went back to it.

" It's just part-time care," he continued. "What do you think of that? You should be happy about that."

She put down the magazine and began to brighten.

"Kam Douglas will be the caregiver," she said. "Once out of Nancy's house, he can live in the old house with your father. This is cheaper with food for him too, so he can keep his pool job and buy some of his own food, learning his English in spare time. Lodging should be free for him as the caregiver. He can sleep in your old room where you were younger, and he is improving his English living with lawyer, native speaker with college education. He is also spending lot of this time away from Cyril."

"Kam Douglas is a boy. You just told me that."

"He's nineteen now and took care of his own grandfather in Shanghai for almost a month all the time to the end. He knows what to do and is big enough to lift your father into the bathtub. I can help with the cooking– prepare dishes here, and Kam Douglas can heat things up if he has to. I will just have to wait a little longer for the furniture."

In bed that night she was still pleasant. He did not raise the question, but she assured him his parents' twin beds— whenever that day would be– would make no difference when he wanted her. At breakfast the next morning she smiled at him, and he felt more generous himself.

"As soon as Kam Douglas moves in with your father," he told her, "I'll have all the home movies transferred to DVD. I'll take everything down to Monte's Video and have them do it. I'll pay for it, and Dad will be able to watch the movies whenever he wants. We'll all get together at the old house and watch them. I'll buy him a DVD player, and Kam Douglas can put in the discs for him until he learns how to do it himself."

"I'll take care of everything with Kam Douglas," she said. "He's good with electric devices. They all are at his age. Mechanical genius."

She did follow through, and when she finally introduced Dana to Kam Douglas there seemed nothing to worry about. The well-fed young man seemed big enough to lift Mr. Watmaugh in and out of a wheel chair, in and out of a bath, and tuck him in at night. His English was not very good, but he had a cheerful, positive attitude—He responded with "Can do" to every question Dana asked. And Erica reassured them she would visit every day with dinner, or at least once a week with several dinners prepared for the freezer.

Dana followed through as well, and within a week Monte himself called from the video store to say the family film archive, now transferred to six convenient discs, was ready to be picked up. Kam Douglas appeared for further instructions, and Dana asked him to swing by Monte's for the discs and the originals on his commute to the Arlington house.

"Mr. Watmaugh is back home now," he told Kam Douglas. "Watch one disc with him when you get there, just one to start, perhaps something from our earlier childhood, a welcome home present for him."

"Can do," Kam Douglas said, and he made a rubbing motion with his fingers.

"Already paid for," Dana said. "Just pick up please."

"Can do."

"Perhaps I'm talking too fast. You put in disc in the DVD player I got for father and hooked up to his TV, and you watch movie on disc with father. Erica and I will be over later with dinner and some for freezer."

"Can do, no problem."

"Tell Monte or whoever the name—Watmaugh, Dana this, Victor that, childhood, bicycles, birthdays, Halloween, and so on. They are expecting you to pick them up. Six discs."

"Victor and childhood. No problem."

"Victor is grown up now. Just say Watmaugh." He handed Kam Douglas an index card with the family name printed in block letters. "They are expecting you. Call me if there is a problem."

"No problem. Victor is grown up."

Kam Douglas followed through as best he could. This meant taking Cyril with him to Monte's Video.

"It's hard name for spelling and pronouncing," he said to Cyril after parking the truck in front of the store. "Written down here."

"Watmaugh," Cyril said. "I know it. What's the first name?"

"Victor."

"Victor Watmaugh. What the fuck, Victor Watmaugh the divorce lawyer in McLean?"

"He's grown up now."

"He's a dip shit is what he is. Last year that dick head fucked up my Mom's divorce so bad she got no alimony, just fucking child support she has to use for rent and shit. And he's still making her pay his fucking bill—thirty dollars a month every fucking month for five years or some such shit. And we're here to do what?"

"Pick up old movies. Victor grown up now."

"Just leave it to me. Wait here."

Kam Douglas was content to wait, and when Cyril climbed back in the truck and handed him one disc, not six, he did not object.

"It's all on one disc," Cyril said. The fucking idiot at the counter had the order all fucked up. He gave me six discs instead of one, and he was expecting me to take back a crate full of film cans and shit, but I told him to throw it all out—'Throw all that shit out, I want a refund'– and he starts to go fucking ballistic, so I had to take something else from the store to calm him down. Then I had to walk out the back with all that shit in the crate and throw everything in the dumpster on my own. No refund, but I sent a message. This DVD here is a classic"—he held up a budget Hollywood feature in a thin box—"cost me three bucks out of pocket because this Monte or whoever he's like picking up the fucking phone to call your Victor and looking at me. But, see, I'm telling him I've got what you want, because it's got Victor's name on it, Victor all grown up, and he says just take it too, so I'm thinking I can send a message to your dip shit friend in McLean, a message for Victor fucking Watmaugh– All Grown Up."

Kam Douglas nodded at what seemed the gist of the explanation, but he had his doubts about showing up with just the one disc. He said part of the same to his elderly charge later in the day when he put the disc in the player, tried to explain something about it showing Victor all grown up, and outlined a procedure for operating the player.

"A message film, you say," the old man said. "Jesus H. Christ. Can't we watch the Sports Channel or maybe Jeopardy? I feel ready for Jeopardy."

"Your son and someone else say better off watching the message. Son is over here at night with Erica and they're bringing dinner. They will ask about it, and I can't understand everything. Help me out and I help you out. This movie is about your home, a home movie. Victor is in it."

"Victor is in it. Jesus, wake me when it's over. No, don't wake me. Let me die peacefully."

But to Kam Douglas's peace of mind Mr. Watmaugh stayed awake and alert throughout the film. The feature was not three generations of home movies but *Kiss of*

Death with Victor Mature and Richard Widmark. Thanks to Dr. Flores, Mr. Watmaugh remembered seeing it as a boy on first release in 1947, and he was eager to share the memory with his new caretaker. Kam Douglas was well into his third bowl of popcorn and smiled politely.

"My father took me to see it," he said. "I was nine. Mother was visiting Grandma Celeste in Fredericksburg. She had taken the Saturday morning train down there but left dinner for us in the icebox, leg of lamb, which I never liked much but was able to eat with the mint jelly and the baked potato. After dinner, my father and I rode the streetcar downtown to the old Warner Theatre off Pennsylvania Avenue, just the two of us. My first time there– It was a huge theatre, and the movie had started. The usher, a tall, pretty redhead in a uniform and a little hat, led us to our seats with a flashlight because the place was so big and dark. The movie was in black and white, as you saw, and they were so dark in those days. The plot was hard for me to follow, too old for me then. I thought there would be kissing and then someone would die as a result, a kiss with poison lipstick or incurable germs. I did not understand that a kiss of death meant betrayal, someone close to you betraying you. I did not know that word, betrayal, but I could tell the Mature character was not all bad, and I knew Widmark the gangster was hopeless after he kicked the old lady in the wheelchair down the stairs and laughed at her. Do you understand any of this?"

"I can, yes– Must try my best to resist any such temptation in caretaking. But sometimes it is very difficult for me having patience with old people, slow kind of people not in right mind and bad tempered, people too long living."

"Me too, and don't get me going about my boys. Back then, I just wanted the picture to be over, but it wasn't, and my father leans over and whispers to me, 'I have to make a phone call. I'll be back in a few minutes.' He sold insurance, life insurance, house, car, and he had to call people to sell it, even at night. He stands up and leaves his hat on the seat, but then he remembers something important, bends over and whispers in my ear again– 'Don't let anyone sit next to you while I'm gone. And don't let anyone sit on my hat.' Then he disappears into the darkness. Now I'm frightened of this movie I don't understand very well, and the darkness, the vast, dark theatre, the harsh and difficult dialogue of the actors, the somber music, the violence, the pervasive unhappiness. And I'm frightened at the prospect of someone strange sitting next to me, someone menacing, a large man who might bother me, or maybe someone who is going to sit on the hat because it's dark and he can't see it there on the seat. I was just nine. My father is gone a long time, and I've lost any sense of the movie. I look down the aisle wondering where he is and at the same time worrying about someone else showing up. Then it actually happens. It all comes to life. Someone, a large, shadowy figure who can't possibly be my father starts down the aisle toward me, and I pick up the hat. But then I realize picking up the hat is like inviting the stranger to sit down next to me. I don't know what the hell to do. I put the hat back on the seat, pick it up again, put it back— and the man sits down on it. 'Sorry,' he says, gets up and continues down the aisle. Now I have the hat in my hands, and I can tell it's ruined– a perfect, neatly blocked, fedora hat that businessmen wore in those days, even when they were just going to the movies with their boy. And now it's ruined. I try to give it some shape, but I can't do anything with it. It's hopeless. I close my eyes, and when I open them I'm looking up at the screen again, but now I see a shadow moving across it—This time it's my father starting down the aisle toward me . . ."

Kam Douglas put his hand on Mr. Watmaugh's shoulder–

"Enough," he said. "Stop. Erica is here with Dana. Be distracting from any business problems about Monte's Video and how many discs. No, maybe not distracting, maybe worse thing all over. Not saying anything is maybe best for family harmony."

Mr. Watmaugh did not ask Kam Douglas what these business problems might be or what the problem at Monte's Video– which he took to be a city in South America—was all about. Dinner conversation, however, took a turn toward discovery when Dana brought up the subject of special days and events in the old house– Birthday parties in this very dining room, around this very table, his parties and Victor's—once even a joint birthday party since their special days were just a month apart. Dana was the only one with a drink, a third glass of white wine, and Erica had brought a chocolate layer cake for dessert.

"Victor raised a stink about sharing a birthday party," he said. "I didn't mind it myself. I was ten and he was little more than a year older. I looked up to him, not because he was older and bigger but because I thought he had a certain magnanimity somewhere deep inside him, a big brother trait that would come out when it really counted. That's what I thought then."

He sighed and laughed at his lost ingenuousness, then looked at Erica as if for confirmation. She got up from the table, gathered plates and silverware and took them into the kitchen. He turned to his father sitting in his wheelchair, then looked at Kam Douglas seated next to the old man as if expecting one of them to say something. They had no more to say than Erica did, so he brought the conversation into the present.

"What did you two think of all that ancient footage? How much did you get through?"

"We saw good part of it," Kam Douglas said right away. "Good movie, not everyone in it all bad, just one all bad."

"I do know what you mean," Dana said, "though perhaps that is an observation better left to the immediate family. When I hear you say it, I'm put in an awkward position. I know you mean well."

"Thanks for passing it on to us," Mr. Watmaugh said. "Thoughtful of you, both of you. You are both good boys."

"It's meant for you," Dana said. "That's why I ordered it." He filled his glass again.

"You know," Mr. Watmaugh continued, "seeing it again I understand it better, a lot better. Some good insights do come with age. I even see a theme, something I did not have a word for when I was younger."

"I suppose you mean something about Victor," Dana said.

"If you want to put it that way."

"How would you put it?"

He raised his arm and pointed to a sign in air– "Betrayal." He put his arm down. "I never understood it until now—this kiss of death from someone you trusted, an ingrate, a remorseless sociopath really, someone who deserves everything he gets, or doesn't get, I should say– eventually. It's biblical, I guess."

Dana was taken aback at what he heard. True, his brother was no doubt wealthy enough already—but his own father disowning Victor, the first- born– He tried to say No to the old man, but he felt tears and the word caught in his throat.

"I should not have brought it up," Dana managed to say before starting to weep. He got up quickly—"to help Erica in the kitchen."

But when he saw her at the sink rinsing plates, he turned away, walked down the hall and ended up in his old bedroom. The room was dark, but he did not turn on the light. He bumped into the closet doors against the wall, and a layer of shoeboxes tumbled down, spilling photographs onto the floor. He felt for them with his hands, then sat down on the floor. He could make out the two beds by the gray light of the window, and he thought about what it meant to be the sole heir of his father's estate, how his life would change into something magnificent, how ecstatic Erica would be when he told her, and whether having a swimming pool was more trouble than it was worth.

Dinner over, Kam Douglas pushed Mr. Watmaugh into the living room then went back to the table to collect napkins and glasses for the kitchen. Erica sent him to fetch Dana—

"He'll be in one of the bedrooms," she said, "and I have something to say to both of you."

Dana had not quite recovered but returned with Kam Douglas and pretended to listen to her.

"I've put five dinners in the freezer," she said drying her hands. "When you're over here next time all you have to do is heat them up in the microwave. Kam Douglas, you can do it but don't try cooking anything on the stovetop or have any kind of alcohol to drink– I'll hear about it and tell your mother. If Cyril shows up, don't let him in the house and don't go anywhere with him. I will find out."

Kam Douglas nodded and smiled, and Dana looked up at the ceiling. Clean up remained brisk and quiet, and none too soon the four of them were gathered at the front door, chorusing how well everything had worked out with Mr. Watmaugh– happy, surely, to be back in his own domain. Dana, now composed, feeling more than generous, held out a folded twenty- dollar bill for Kam Douglas and told him how important it was to choose his friends, the right kind of friends, if he wanted to get somewhere in this country. Mr. Watmaugh did not seem to notice this gesture but turned to Erica and motioned for her to bend close to him. He had something to tell her that he did not want Dana to hear.

"My bedroom set," he whispered close to her ear, "the two beds, the two dressers, the writing desk—I want you to take them, you and Dana, but don't tell him just yet. Tell him when you get home. No, wait. Don't ruin the rest of your evening. Tell him in two or three days. I have to touch base with Victor first, but he won't want that old furniture. He's happily married and has a fine bedroom set, a big bed, four poster, large night tables, two beautiful dressers, what you call colonial style, highboys. Their bedroom has a sitting area, easy chairs, all very nice furniture, and a large walk-in closet. The master bathroom has a big tub, a spa type with jets, and a separate shower stall, a large one with two nozzles. Two people could use it at the same time. Believe me, he won't want to bother with a twin bed set."

"Where will you sleep?"

"I'll have Kam Douglas haul the old set over to your place. He's a good boy, you know. I have a new set on order, a double or queen- sized bed, I forget which, a new dresser, night tables, a big TV cabinet like you see in a hotel. Everything will be here soon, maybe next week. I'm not sure of the day."

"You don't like your old bed anymore, and your wife's?"

"In those days twin beds seemed more fashionable, more respectable or something. Heather wanted twin beds. I never liked the arrangement, always wanted a bigger bed, a double. In some ways, you remind me of her as a younger woman."

"Thank you, Mr. Watmaugh," she said, and kissed him on the cheek.

"Just call me Victor," he said, "and you never know, I might get lucky."

George McLoone

If I could remember you

What may have been different
Had those first, child like hopes
Been realized?

Would I be in a
Better state
If tonight, under that ancient white
Moon
You were sitting on my couch, smiling
Like I
Always knew you
Could?
Would things be different or just
Different If we had danced,
Even for an hour
Under the lights
In that small, mid-western town?

Frank Terry

Drive

Sandy closed the door on Martha Baker's kid. He hadn't realized Keven had gotten so big, though he was the same age as Sandy's own son.

"What'd you do that for?" Muddy's voice had to shoulder its way up from beneath the carriage of an '84 Corolla. By the time it crossed the ventilation fan to Sandy, it was a weak noise easy enough to ignore. Sandy stretched his neck to get a kink out before returning to the transmission of the '82 Dakota, perched on the garage's only lift.

Muddy slid his creeper to get his head clear of the car and spoke with exaggerated enunciation. "Why did you shut the door in the kid's face?"

Sandy sprayed some WD-40 on the u-bolts he had to loosen to slide the drive shaft back. When the mist settled, he looked up. "A kid his age don't need to be fencing for Joey O."

Muddy reached for a socket wrench. "The kid's working hard. He's trying to make something of hisself."

"Better ways to do it."

Muddy shoved himself back under the Corolla. Sandy tried the bolts again. One was still stuck, so he let out a habitual curse. Muddy wheeled himself back out. "Exactly how is he supposed to make something of hisself right now? In this economy?"

Sandy shrugged. "This ain't the only case of times being hard."

"You're awful holy of a sudden. It's not like you don't buy hot parts."

"Not from kids I don't." Sandy wiped his hands on the nearest rag before picking up his wrench again.

Muddy rolled back under the carriage. The men worked in silence for a few minutes, save for the occasional muttering at the intransience of bolts or other parts. Before long, Muddy reemerged.

"Hey Sandy, you hear that the pope is making a new saint?"

"Nope." Sandy wiped his hands again without looking at Muddy.

"Ya, Saint Arthur Sands. Saint Sandy. The only kicker is you have to die first."

"That so?"

"That's so. But since you ain't dead yet, you may as well give the kid a break. Just buy a few damn parts from him. Keven's a good kid in spite of his mother."

"I never said he wasn't. Matter of fact, I got no problem with Martha." He soaked the bolt again and turned his attention to inspecting the bell housing cover.

"A lot of men don't," Muddy snorted. "You one of the mystery fathers?"

"Nope."

"Six kids and not one man to stick around. Three of the kids don't even know who their dad is. I expect Martha don't know neither."

"Sounds like a situation I want to stay clear of."

"What do you do for sex anyway?"

"I don't tell you, that's what."

"That's true. You never have. Don't know what I'd do in your situation."

"I do all right." Sandy went back to the shelf and found a flathead screwdriver.

Muddy watched him. "Keven ain't getting the parts hisself. He's just working for Joey O. It's like an apprenticeship."

Sandy laughed. "Becoming a carpenter is like an apprenticeship. Working for Joey O. is like going to jail."

The side door opened, bringing the cold fresh air and a carbon copy of Sandy, minus the wrinkles and knotted neck. "Who's going to jail?"

"Nobody's going to jail Sandbox, we're just talking about kids these days." Muddy got up to daub some debris out of his eye.

"Kids these days," the boy intoned solemnly. "Why when I was younger, we knew how to work."

"That's what I'm talking about!" laughed Muddy, blinking "Sandy, there ain't nothing wrong with this exhaust. Esther swears it's running loud, but I looked it up and down, and you heard it run. What you want me to do?"

Sandy watched his son cross the garage to the third bay, reserved for the 1968 Mustang restoration project that was supposed to be a father-son experience. When they finished it, they would sell the car to pay for the portion of college not covered by scholarships. By the time Sandy had worked on cars all day, his body could hardly stand another minute with wrench in hand. But Artie kept on track to have it finished before he left for university in the fall. The boy was so focused. He came home from practice—currently basketball—then grabbed a sandwich and worked on the car for a couple hours, did his homework, called his girlfriend, and went to bed. Weekends he worked at the corner store, went out with Shelly or friends and came home on time.

"I could replace the header pipe, it'll probably go in another year or so," Muddy suggested. "If we tell her nothing's wrong, she'll just take it someplace else."

Sandy loaded himself on the creeper and slid under the corolla with a trouble light. He looked up and down the exhaust and rolled back out. "If Esther is this fussy about her car, I can only imagine what her doctor bills are like. Don't replace the pipe, just put on a new heat shield and charge her 20 minutes labor."

Muddy rooted around in the store room for a minute. "Damnitall, we don't have the right OEM."

"That's all right, I'll get them tomorrow. It's time for you to hit it anyway."

Muddy reemerged from the store room and glanced at the clock. It was only quarter till. "Right-o. Don't forget about the package that came for Sandbox."

"My clutch kit?" Artie practically squeaked with excitement. Sandy wanted to take that pure childish joy and flash freeze it. His son was mostly a young man now, but in moments like this still a child in the best sense of the word.

"Don't know. Open it." Sandy pointed with his wrench toward the box on the bench along the side of the garage.

Muddy lathered with Lava soap up to his elbows. He rinsed down, then rubbed his arms with brown paper towel. “Hey Sandbox, you know Keven Baker?”

Artie cut open the sealing tape with his pocket knife. “Sure. Why?”

“He a good guy?”

“Ya, real good guy. His mom, now, is another story. She actually wants him to drop out of school so he can get a second job. You believe that?”

Muddy tsked. “That’s a shame. You’d think she has enough time to get pregnant every year, she ought to be able to find the time to get a steady job herself.”

Artie pulled back the top flaps. “Oh she works, but she’s like he’s not going to college or anything, so he may as well get a jump on the job market. She doesn’t get it that things have changed. You can’t get a decent job without a high school diploma anymore.”

“So true.” Muddy pulled off his garage shoes. “I sure hope someone gives that kid a break sometime.” He slipped his clean shoes on. “Good night. See you tomorrow Saint Sandy.”

Artie sliced open the interior packaging and pulled out the 9” three-puck ceramic racing clutch. “Yes!” He sounded like he had just won the lottery.

“You know how that goes in?”

“I bet the two of us can figure it out,” Artie grinned.

*****

Keven Baker strode from Sandy's Auto Repair, shame burning in his cheeks. If Sandy's creepy sidekick hadn't been there, maybe he could have gotten a break. But Muddy had it in for his whole family ever since he came sniffing around his mother's door and got turned away like a cur. Men always thought his mom would be eager and willing, but she hadn't been that way for years. He could only imagine all the things Muddy had said against him.

Keven had washed dishes for the last couple years for minimum wage. When one of his co-workers started stealing parts for Joey O., Keven said he'd like to try fencing as a way to make money for college. He hadn't given up on the possibility of college, though his mother had already told him she wouldn't sign any loans for him. She couldn't see the point in education, but he couldn't see any other point. It was one of the few areas of contention between them.

Joey O. had wanted him steal the cars or their parts, but Keven wasn't stupid. He knew Joey O. liked to have the younger kids do that because they didn't do hard time, but he wasn't about get grand theft auto on his record even as a juvenile. Selling hot parts was colorful, but stealing cars branded yourself as hard core. He stood his ground, and Joey O. got a kick out of that. Said he'd rather have a smart kid like Keven keep his hands clean anyway and he gave him a circuit.

Sandy's Auto Repair wasn't on the circuit. His shop had different suppliers, but Joey O. told Keven that if he could open up a few new markets he would get a big bonus. Enough to cover the first semester's textbooks. It stood to reason that Sandy would be willing to doing business with Keven. His son was the same age as him and he had heard Sandy stick up for his mom once or twice. But that was before Muddy had come nosing around their house and undoubtedly poisoning Sandy's mind.

Of course, Muddy might not have been the only problem. Maybe Sandy's son Artie was in the mix too. Keven had plenty of reason to resent Artie, but up until now he had made up his mind to be a bigger person than to harbor petty resentments. His mother taught him that.

Two years ago Keven's girlfriend Shelly had dumped him and before long she was going steady with Artie—she called him Arthur. Artie was the golden child of the dingy little suburb. He was homecoming king, an all-around athlete, straight-A student, and bound to the University of Pennsylvania in the fall. On top of this, he was mechanically gifted, making all the girls swoon when he went on and on about his Mustang. But in spite of his status as the Anointed One, he had always been friendly to Keven. Other popular kids ignored Keven or put him down because he didn't have nice clothes or because he was so close to his mother. But Artie wasn't like that. He was a good guy. So it had seemed.

Sandy must have his reasons for turning Keven away. Maybe Artie had been making fun of him all along. Working on that beautiful car with his dad and talking about how Shelly used to date a loser named Keven Baker. Artie and Muddy probably sat around making lewd jokes about his mom and Sandy was right there with him.

Keven knew more than one way to get the money he needed. He had to meet Joey O. tonight to settle accounts. He may not have earned the bonus, but he could earn bigger commissions by selling higher quality parts.

Joey O. usually conducted business in the backroom of his cousin's tavern, but the underage crowd met him in the ice cream shop next door.

"Want a shake?"

"Naw, just a coffee," Keven replied.

"Two coffees, please." Joey O. handed four dollars to the girl at the counter and dumped the change in the tip jar. He and Keven slid into an isolated booth in the back.

Keven gave Joey O. the inventory sheet and the revenue from the sales. Joey O. counted out Keven's commission. "This working out okay for you Keven?"

"Sure."

"No new markets though?"

"Not yet." He sipped the coffee. "What kind of market do you think there is for vintage parts?"

"Vintage car parts? You kidding? That's a great market. Complicated, but great. Why?"

"I was trying to make a sale at Arthur Sand's shop. He wasn't buying, but as we were talking I got a good look at his security system." He set the mug down and looked right at Joey O. "It's a joke."

Joey O. looked at him. "And?"

"You don't know about his 1968 Mustang? It's in the third bay of the garage."

Joey O. sat back with narrowed eyes. "Is that so?"

"That's so."

"You change your mind about getting your hands dirty then?"

"No I haven't. Tell the truth, I'd appreciate you let me know when you send someone to do it because I want to have a rock solid alibi that night."

Joey O. stirred his coffee, then pointed the plastic stirrer at him. "You are a smart kid. We'll get you to college yet."

"I get to fence the parts?"

"It's more complicated than what you've done, but you can learn."

Keven and Artie ended up at the same party Saturday night. That was just like Artie. The most popular kid in school, but he'd go to a party full of burnouts and nobodies just because he was invited. Artie drank, but not a lot. "I'm driving," he said and the kid who offered him the second beer nodded as if he himself would not be driving. Keven didn't touch drink. His mother had taught him that it corrupted men and he never found any evidence to contradict her.

Shelly was overly nice to him like she always was, but Artie was just normal. Keven meant to be in a crowd, to be seen away from the scene of the crime, but he hadn't meant to actually be speaking to Artie as Joey O.'s henchmen broke into Sandy's shop and hauled away the Mustang. He kept trying to catch the eye of someone—anyone—who would call him across the room. Instead, he had to answer all Artie's attentive questions about school, work, family. "What about you, Artie. You excited to get out to Philly this fall?" If Keven couldn't avoid conversation, he may as well plunge headlong.

"Sure, I mean if it all works out."

"What's not to work out? They let you in, you accepted. It's all go, right?"

"I still have to finish the car and sell it."

"Sell it? I thought you loved that car."

Artie's face took on a glow. "You know I love that car. 1968 was such a great year for the Mustang, and it's actually really cool to work on it with my dad. But the whole plan was to restore it, then sell it for my tuition. At least my first year, after that I need to find more scholarships."

Keven gaped. He couldn't formulate his thoughts. He had to say something, so he stammered, "What?"

Artie laughed, "Which part?"

Keven forced his mouth into a smile, "Sorry, it's loud in here. You said you are finding more scholarships?"

"Yeah, or maybe we'll restore another car next summer. I don't know. It'll all work out."

"Well, hey, good luck with that man." Keven punched him lightly in the shoulder and made his way through the crowd. He had to leave, get some air. Except that he had to stay here, in the crowd. In the alibi.

The days were getting longer, but the sun still wasn't up when Sandy opened the shop on Monday. He switched on the small fluorescent lamp above the desk. He didn't like to flood the place with light until he was ready for business. But even in the dim glow, he noticed something not right. When he threw the full lights on, he stared at an empty spot where the Mustang had been. He crossed the garage, crouched down, touched the air where the tires should have been, and sank to the oily cement.

By the time Muddy arrived, the cops were already there.

"Sandy?"

"I'm going to kill him."

"Who?"

"That Baker kid. Keven. I swear to God I will kill him." Muddy looked past Sandy's tight face to the place the convertible used to be.

"Sandy."

"I'm serious, Muddy."

Muddy leaned in close and whispered, "Could you be just a little less serious about it until the cops leave?"

Sandy stalked out. Muddy hailed the older cop.

"Jimbo."

Jimbo shook his head. "I never seen Sandy like that. He was going apeshit when we got here. If you're his friend I'd keep close to him, make sure he doesn't do anything stupid."

"Any idea who did this?"

"Sandy says Martha Baker's kid, but wouldn't say why he thought that. I tried to tell him that there are a million people who could have wanted that car. We're taking prints now and we'll see. I'd keep Sandy away from this kid if I were you."

"Yeah, cuz he always listens to what I have to say." He shook his head. "When do you think they broke in?"

Jimbo shrugged. "Don't know yet. Could have been any time between when you closed up on Saturday afternoon and when Sandy got here this morning. Hard to say. Listen, I got to finish this up here."

"Sure, I'll catch up with you later."

Muddy stepped outside next to Sandy. He lit a cigarette.

"You talk to insurance yet?"

"Ya."

"What'd they say?"

"They'll get back to me."

"What's the problem?"

"My business was insured. The Mustang was not part of my business."

"Bullshit. You were planning to sell it weren't you?"

"It's in Artie's name. He was gonna sell it."

"That's some bureaucratic bullshit." Muddy exhaled a stream of smoke.

"The money ain't the point. Not the whole point."

"I know. You tell him yet?"

"Nope."

The younger cop poked his head out. "Mr. Sands? We're about to finish up here. Here's my card, give me a call any time. We'll talk to Keven Baker and let you know how it goes."

"Okay, thanks."

As the cruiser headed down the street, Muddy changed his shoes. "Well, I guess I'll call in the order for Eshter's heat shield. They didn't take anything off her car did they?"

"Nope. Nothing but the Mustang."

"You need me to call in anything else?"

"I don't think I'm going to work today. Close up shop at the end of the day, will ya?"

"Sandy, wait a minute. Where are you going?"

"And don't touch that transmission I was working on." Sandy grabbed his jacket as he stormed out the door. Before Muddy even crossed the garage to follow him, Sandy peeled out of the lot.

Muddy stared at the place where the Mustang had been. He crossed to the desk and thumbed through the phone book. He picked up the receiver and dialed. "Hello Martha? It's Mark Reynolds…I'm doing all right. I'm calling about your son Keven…He's fine, but I think he may have gotten mixed up in something. At least Sandy thinks so…Sandy, Arthur Sands, from Sandy's Auto Repair…Ya, his son had a Mustang he was restoring, and this weekend someone broke in and …I'm not saying it was Keven, I'm just trying to tell you that's what Sandy thinks and for all I know he's headed over there now…Whatever you think best, I just wanted to let you know is all…Okay bye."

Sandy watched the kids head into school. When he saw Keven Baker, he swung out of his truck. "Keven!" He hollered. The boy pretended he hadn't heard him, so Sandy bellowed "Keven Baker!" That brought him over.

"Keven," he said. "I've been thinking over your offer to sell me a few things. I guess I was wrong. Why don't you come with me and we'll settle up."

Keven's face betrayed everything. "I can't right now, I've got school."

"This shouldn't take long. Don't you want to earn you commission?"

"I really can't be late for my first hour class. How about I come by after I get off my job tonight?"

"I'll be closed up by then."

"Okay, tomorrow then." Keven was sweating.

Sandy grabbed him by the collar. "I don't think so." He tried to shove him into the cab, but some kids shouted for a teacher and a crowd gathered. Artie came running.

"Dad? What's going on?"

"Keven, you want to tell Artie what's going on?" He shoved the kid against the car. "Huh? You want to tell him why I'm here?"

Keven was shaking. "Artie, your dad wants to buy some parts from me. I told him I had school and he—"

"What kind of parts, Keven? Do you want to tell Artie what kind of parts you happen to have for sale right now?"

"What kind?" Keven gulped.

"Dad, it's all right. Keven, are you okay?"

"You must have a lot of parts right now for a 19-fucking-68 Mustang! Don't you?" He banged Keven repeatedly against the door.

The gym teacher trotted up and spoke in a quiver. "Mr. Sands, we've called the police. Let Keven go."

Sandy turned Keven and acted like he was going to release him, but as he spun the boy away, he landed a blow to his face. Keven half ducked and half fell to the ground but jumped back up, blood streaming from his nose. He tried to get a jab to Sandy's gut, but the older man caught his arm and twisted it around till he heard a popping sound. Keven was now completely incapacitated, but Sandy hauled his foot back to deliver a parting kick anyway. "Tell Joey O. he shouldn't hire stupid little shits like you."

Only then did he look at his son, whose innocent face seemed ready to crumple. "Come on, we have to go to the shop." Artie moved towards the truck, but the gym teacher put a hand on his arm.

"Artie, you need to stay here until the police arrive." When the boy allowed himself to be held in place by the teacher, Sandy shrugged as if it didn't matter to him, slid into the truck, and pulled away. In the rearview mirror he saw his son kneel over Keven.

Sandy hadn't been to his river spot for years. When his wife had left him and Artie, he used to go there all the time. He'd let Muddy run the shop while he sat on the bank for hours on end. There were plenty of places to sit along the river bank, but this was his spot. He never fished from it and never showed it to another soul. He'd just sit there and let the river wash all his anger away. The anger built up again when he would return home and see all the reminders of her. He would cook for Artie, and wash the dishes, and give him a bath. All the things his wife was supposed to do. Early the next day, he would have to go to the river again.

Now he knew he should have come here first. He should have never gone to the school. Should have never beat up Keven Baker in front of his son. But how else can you respond when someone comes into your shop to steal your son's dreams? When he thought about Keven stealing from his son, only the pull of the river kept him from getting up to kill the kid. Artie was the nicest smartest person he had ever known. He could never figure out how this child belonged to a lousy grease monkey like himself. Why would anyone ever want to hurt someone like that? For a few measly bucks? Sandy pictured himself beating Keven's head with a pipe, but threw the image out of his head to let the river carry it downstream.

He guessed the police were at his shop again by now. Muddy would probably mess the situation further by making some crazy lie to protect Sandy. Nothing he could do about any of it now except to watch the river flow.

Artie didn't come home that night. He left a message saying he would sleep on the couch at Shelly's house. Sandy called Shelly's parents and asked if Artie could continue to stay there until he found out what his bail would be. They said of course and he thanked them. Then he thanked the officers for letting him work that out before they took him away.

Muddy fixed everything with a bondsman so that Sandy was back home by sunup the next morning. He was catching a nap in the recliner when the phone rang.

"Arthur?"

"Yes, who's this?"

"It's Martha Baker."

"Martha." He knew he knew her, but he had just been dreaming about the shop and was trying to connect her name to a customer. Then he remembered. "Oh. Martha."

"That all you can say?"

"I don't know. I think I might not supposed to be in contact with you."

"Lawyer tell you that?"

"Lawyer? No." Talking to a lawyer was on his to do list today.

"Cops?"

"Cops what?"

"Cops tell you not to talk to me?"

"I honestly don't even know."

There was a pause on the line.

"They arrested Keven."

"Oh."

"Why do they—why do you think he took that car? He never done nothing like that before."

"I maybe shouldn't say why."

"Lawyer again?"

"Not exactly. That why you're calling? To find out whether I'm lawyered up?"

"Something like that."

"Well, not yet. I'm working on it."

"Arthur, we've known each other a long time. I know we've never been close, but we go back to the old neighborhood in the city. Our folks go back longer than that."

"I know." He was trying to figure out if that mattered in this situation. It hadn't occurred to him that it might.

"Not that you're asking, but Keven's going to be okay."

Sandy clenched his teeth, forming various replies and then picturing them floating away in the river. When she didn't say anything further, he forced out an innocuous, "Is that so?"

"Ya," she said softly, "I think that's so. I don't know about that shoulder, but the doctor says he's young enough that it can heal."

"Well, I guess I'm probably not supposed to be talking with you."

"Arthur, you are in this a lot deeper than he is. All the same, I don't want to see my boy going down the wrong road."

He took a breath. "Okay. So?"

"What if you pay for his doctor bills and neither of us press charges?"

"He going to pay for the Mustang?"

"He didn't have nothing to do with that."

"That what he says?"

She didn't reply.

"Martha, does Keven deny it?"

"He's protecting somebody! I know he is!"

"Of course he is. Joey O. don't pick out squealers to run his jobs for him. You know that."

"I don't know nothing about that. He's a good kid."

"Artie's a good kid."

"I never said he wasn't."

"That car was Artie's, not mine."

"If Keven's responsible, he'll pay."

"Let me think about it Martha."

"Okay, but not too long."

"I know. Thanks for calling Martha." He put the phone down and sunk back into something resembling sleep.

When he woke he called Shelly's parents and they said Artie would like to stay with them for a bit. He apologized but they said it was no trouble, that he was almost like a son to them.

Keven tried to believe his mother when she enthusiastically assured him that his shoulder would heal and that his nose looked better than ever with that slightly disjointed look. The doctor had used words like "probably" and "likelihood" instead of his mother's "definitely" and "absolutely." Still, no point in believing he wouldn't heal. He had to look forward.

Though he loved his mother dearly, he had the sense to make the most of the hand now dealt to him. When he pointed out he couldn't work if he wanted the shoulder to heal properly, he played up the amount of pain he was in. She agreed to cosign his student loans. He tried to feel glad about it, but something more oppressive than lack of education had begun to take hold of him. He couldn't look in most people's eyes anymore. He noticed it first when his mother asked him if he had been responsible. He looked away when he denied it. Then later he looked away when he said he was the one to break in. After that he realized he was avoiding his younger brothers and sisters, even though he had always been close with them. He thought the one person he could look in the eyes was Joey O., but he knew better than to attempt any contact with him and no longer wanted to anyway.

His mother had worked things out. Sandy would put money into an escrow account that could only be used for Keven's medical bills. Meanwhile, Keven would set up another account to pay for the Mustang. The deal had to be signed and notarized and lawyers had to get their cut. He had wanted to just affix his signature to the necessary forms and mail them wherever they needed to go, but his mother insisted that he meet Artie face to face and apologize before signing. She would make sure Sandy wasn't there if he wanted, but he said it was all right.

He tried to dress up, but he couldn't afford to slice up his nice clothes to accommodate his shoulder. So he put on dress pants, cut a t-shirt to fit around the brace, then draped a sports coat over that. The effect was of an unimpressive Don Johnson in a lot of pain. When he entered the lawyer's office, he thought he saw Artie fight down a smile at the getup. Keven looked away.

The lawyer ushered them all into a small conference room where she had the papers arranged. When they were settled, Keven looked directly at his classmate. "Artie," he said, "I just want you to know that I am really sorry. I knew how much that car meant to you, but I didn't know it was paying for your college education." Suddenly , the exhaustion, fear, and pain he'd been through took charge and he was appalled to find he was choking up. This was hardly the manful apology he had envisioned. He tried to plunge ahead, "I would have never done what I did if I had known." It was no good. Out of nowhere, his mouth started twitching. Keven couldn't think of the last time he cried. He wrapped up as fast as he could. "Anyway, I'm sorry."

Everyone in the room stared at the two boys. Artie stretched his hand across the table. "Apology accepted Keven. My grandparents are helping me out with tuition for this year until you can pay me back. It's going to work out." Martha nudged her son who didn't realize Artie was trying to shake his hand. He extended his good left arm in an awkward motion that was a close approximation of a handshake. The room sighed in relief. All eyes turned expectantly to Sandy.

"Keven," Sandy started flatly, "I apologize for what I did. I hope you understand I was only reacting that way because I love my son so much." Now it was Sandy's turn to lose control of his voice. "I just wanted everything to be perfect for him." A long pause ensued in which Sandy started to work his mouth several times. He finally got his vocal chords under his command again, and though he was ostensibly addressing Keven, he was turning now to Artie. "My son is the most wonderful thing that ever happened to me, and I couldn't believe you would want to hurt him. That's why I did what I did. But I know I was wrong and I will never ever forgive myself. I was wrong and I know it. I will always be sorry for what I did."

During the speech, Artie's features lost the softness they held when he forgave Keven and now were locked in a stony motionless gaze fixed on nothing.

Keven supposedly spoke to Sandy, but he too faced Artie. "I accept your apology Mr. Sands. I can understand how you lost your temper. Artie is lucky to have a father who thinks so much of him." Artie still stared fixedly at the wall. Silence saturated the room until the lawyer pulled packets of paper from her file folders and showed Keven and Sandy each where to sign.

When they put down their pens, they all stood. "I'll see you around school," Artie said.

"Ya, I guess so," replied Keven. He followed the father and son from the room, Artie outpacing his dad. When Artie reached the door, he stepped into Shelly's waiting car without even a glance at Sandy, who suddenly seemed impossibly delicate.

Keven arranged himself uncomfortably in his mother's car and stared morosely out the window at the few patches of green emerging uncertainly from the clutches of winter. "Mom?"

"Ya?"

“I just want you to know that whatever you do, I will always love you.”

She covered his hand with her own. “I know honey. And I will always love you too. No matter what.” She engaged the transmission and each pretended not to look as they drove by Sandy’s car. It was still in park, with the man inside hunched sobbing over the steering wheel.

Gail Francis

Romance Of Time

Watchmaker’s calculated art of divisible lines
Only seconds gone, recovered, reconciled – time
Confess! Sighs, spies, lies – sleepless unhappiness
Watchmaker’s devices, anxieties, deceptiveness
Chronicled surreptitious relentlessness

Watchmaker, oh so smart, moving hands imperceptibly
Only minutes on a lark, a mark, every man’s destinies
Of life, timeless reality, evolved haphazardly?
Watchmaker’s ticking; dialing death demonstratively,
Defines our zeitgeist zigzaggedly

Watchmaker imparts, twelve more, twenty four
Only hours, resounding earthly chores, draped revolving doors
Elastic Mont Blanc, intestate estate, ravaged wolverine, fate
Watchmaker’s delicate; superfluous dates, aging mates
Never my pretty, inveterate pristine state

Watchmaker’s jouled entropy; never polymorphic prose
Our days, love’s repository, hung in eons of glorious tableaus
Sea of timing, love-tides rent, horizon’s bent, and you relent.
Watchmaker’s intent, time’s dent, never heaven sent
Diamond’s movement, another lover’s decent

Watchmaker’s chime, mellifluous crime, a swindler’s rhyme
Only months behind, martyred time, denied love sublime
Back then, known, love binds, inamorata over time redesigns
Watchmaker unwound, crowned tines, read between the

lines
Timed, stemmed love undermines

Watchmaker's chimera, fool's fantasy, restive two-headed paramour
Of years desolate, suffering insubordinate, forever and for more
Seconds, minutes, hours, days, months, years forever drawing blanks
Watchmaker charlatan tick upon watchband, desolate heart sank
Puller of the pranks, love's forever-deceptive mountebank

max keanu

An Unnatural History

What you saw first were their wings.
They were splayed out, pinned to the scrub grass of the back yard. Looking for all the world like a huge hand had swatted them out of the sky and flattened them there.
I saw an owl, two terns, a couple of bright green parakeets, the sad blue smear of a budgerigar and even a southern royal albatross.
I counted at least ten of them lying in the yard. Wings outstretched. Heads turned to greet the weak morning sun. The wind blew a silent downy snowstorm of tiny feathers into the air.
The next thing that you noticed was the smell. A terrible rotten smell that leached up your nose and wouldn't leave. I walked into the yard, my new shoes slung over my neck. They were a size too big for me. My feet throbbed from the packed soil and the wet, red welts the shoes had worn into them.
Ana Maria stood on the broad stone step of the house. She smoked a cigarette and pulled her silk robe around her body. The wind blew golden twists of her hair over her eyes. She looked into the distance, far over the piñero trees and out towards the cliffs and the sea.
I picked my way past six dead racing pigeons arranged in a circle. The sight of pigeons made me panic. I dropped my satchel and ran to Ana-Maria's son, Lucho. He knelt in the thin grass. A small, bony figure short for his ten years. He had tucked his red hair under an outsize woolly hat.
He fluttered in the wind like paper, shivering in his thin cotton shirt and threadbare shorts. His glasses lay in the dust smeared with tears. The lenses were as thick as soda bottles. Ana-Maria's Uncle, Carlos stood a few steps behind him. Lucho's eyes were screwed shut and his face contorted as he pressed it against the small, grey bird in

his hands.
Paloma.
Attached to her was a square of school notebook paper.
"BIRDBOY" it said in red biro.
"Those bastard Gallos," muttered Carlos.
*
The day before, as part of our preparation for the race, Lucho and I had taken Paloma for a training toss. We'd each grasped one of the handles on her wicker basket and carried it to the fields far outside of town. After walking for an hour, we set down the basket in the middle of a copse and opened the lid. Lucho leant into the basket and whispered. Paloma hopped onto the lip.
She was a handsome dark-check hen with gunmetal plumage and dark mottled wings. Her eyes were bright, black and ringed with a band of scarlet. The thin aluminium tag on her left leg marked her out as a racing pigeon. She looked at Lucho and cocked her head. He nodded and she streaked upwards. A ribbon of silver against the rolling clouds.
They had always been like this, even in the delicate days when Paloma resembled nothing more than a ball of fluff drenched in albumen. Lucho had hand-fed her on maize. As soon as she'd grown into a squab, she'd hop onto his shoulders and peck at his hair. After we were sure she'd gone, we walked back towards the town swinging the empty basket between us.
From the road, Paraíso was little more than a huddle of metal-lidded buildings that perched on steep cliffs. British nitrate traders had founded the town in the 18th century. Its fortunes had flourished and withered along with the mining business.
Now, it was a small collection of houses and shops that baked hard like a rock in summer and whose cracked roads were pelted by salt rain during the long, dark Pacific winter.

Carlos always claimed that it was this heritage and the extremes of weather that invested the populace of Paraíso with their twin obsessions: dancing the Cueca on Patriot's day and pigeon racing.

"They dance to keep warm in the winter," he'd say, "and then they sit on their lardy arses watching the pigeons all through summer."

Carlos was waiting for us in the pigeon loft when we arrived. He had built it from pieces of driftwood that he'd sawn into regular shapes and then nailed together. It was painted with an uneven coat of whitewash and its broad opening was covered with a double layer of chicken wire. He sat inside it. An old, raggedy figure perched on one of the three plastic chairs he had rescued from a rubbish tip. Behind him, row upon row of wooden coops lined the wall. Paloma's was in pride of place at the right hand side.

Carlos wore his usual rubber fishing waders and roll-neck sweater. A peaked British naval cap decorated with braid and two intertwined anchors covered his white hair. When I'd asked Lucho how long his Uncle had been at sea for, he'd told me that Carlos had never been to sea in his life, and that the one time that they'd taken the ferry across Lake Rapel his uncle had been sea-sick the whole time.

Carlos pushed back the cap. He scratched the beak of his nose and blew through his drooping moustache.

"She get off, then?" he said.

Lucho nodded and plopped himself down in the chair closest to Paloma's still vacant coop.

"She's the fastest ever, that one," said Carlos. "She's going to beat the Gallo's feathery monsters again. For. Sure." He punctuated the last two words with a clack of his dentures.

"They're bricks. With. Wings"

"Those Gallo's don't respect anyone though. Nasty buggers," Carlos said.

"You're too young to remember this, Augosto," he said, clacking merrily, "but back when Gallo senior was a lad, he and his arseholes broke into Mundez's loft and fed the birds with apples laced with rat poison."
"Some of us have heard this before, you know," said Lucho, affecting a world-weary air and checking the water in the other coops.
Carlos cleared his throat and continued unfazed.
"Thing was, Augosto," he said nodding towards me, "the birds were fine with the apple pieces, but when the rat poison hit the birds bellies, uff! They swelled up like balloons and shrieked like they were on fire. They fell faster than lumps. Of. Rock."
"I tell you, that day it was like it was raining pigeons," said Carlos, with a final clack.
"Yeah, if you believe that sort of thing," said Lucho, winking.
"Why, you cheeky little toad," said Carlos, "that's God's honest truth." He pantomimed boxing Lucho's ears.
*
They had killed Paloma the day before the Copper Company Sweep-stake. The biggest race in the Paraíso calendar. There was still a week to go before the race and without Paloma the Gallos were certain to win.
That evening Lucho and I lay on his roof. Our clothes soaked up the meagre heat from the sheet metal. He wasn't crying anymore, but he wasn't talking much either. The sky was a deep, rich velvet. It was one of those nights when you see the red, gold and blue of the stars. The sort of night where you can scare yourself that you might fall upwards into nothing.
Lucho's cigarette zigged and zagged through the dark. A column of smoke drifted out of his mouth against the broken spine of the Milky Way.
He was not a natural smoker but I had taught him after we'd watched Rooster Cogburn in "True Grit". I'd shown

him how to draw the plumes into his lungs without choking. It was a technique I'd perfected after watching Ana-Maria's disconsolate smoking every morning.

"What's with the hat?" I said, prodding the wool that hid Lucho's long, red hair.

"I'm cold that's all," he said

Lucho shut his eyes and sighed. The stars above vibrated.

"Did you see the note they put on Paloma's body?" he said.

"Yes," I said.

*

I hadn't been there when the thunderbird had come for Lucho in the summer.

My family and I had been on holiday at Valle del Mar when it had happened. I'd arrived home a week after the event, sunburned and full of a strange new energy. I had kissed a girl, while we were away. She'd only been the daughter of the vendedor ambulante who sold ice-creams down at the beach, but I was still eager to get over to Lucho's to smoke illicit cigarettes and relive my conquest.

I unpacked my bag and ran downstairs and tried to slip out of the back door. My mother and the local busybodies huddled around our kitchen-table chattering like monkeys. They were discussing an article in Triunfo.

My mother looked up from the paper and glared at me. I wasn't going over to Lucho's. Not today.

After dinner, I slunk upstairs with the paper. The article was in the corner of the front page. I lay on my bed and read the paper, picking my teeth in the way that I'd seen Carlos do with a wooden tooth-pick.

It told of a boy in our street who had been attacked by a large flying creature while hanging out the laundry. The description of the boy resembled Lucho.

According to the article, the bird had grabbed the boy in its claws and carried him for several streets before

releasing him. He'd fallen to earth in a nearby orchard where a tree had broken his fall.
The attack caused much consternation and confusion in the town. And although the Gallos protested that the whole incident was a scam, they seemed to be gripped by primal anger and fear.
It wasn't long after that they'd started calling Lucho 'Birdboy'.
*
I looked across at him now, lying on the roof. He stared up at the sky, trying to be brave. Below we heard the sound of Carlos as he struggled upstairs impeded by his stiff joints and the evening's rum ration.
"What really happened, with the bird?" I said. Lucho screwed up his eyes and shook his head like he always did.
"This cigarette's going out," he said, passing it to me.
I spat on my fingers and pressed them against the tip, daring myself to hold it until they burned.
"Time to go," Lucho said.
We sat up and slid across the roof. As I did so, I saw a large white cross chalked onto its surface.
"What's that?" I said.
Lucho shrugged and pulled his hat down. He levered himself through the window and back inside.
*
Monday was cold, full of salt sea-mist and gusts of Pacific wind. Lucho was already waiting outside with Ana-Maria when I arrived to walk him to school.
Ana-Maria was younger than the other mothers in our street. She styled her hair into a golden bob that traced the line of her square jaw and thin red lips. For me, her rare smiles possessed felt like the sun coming out.
That morning, like every morning, she stood in the doorway wrapped in her dressing gown. The smell of peppermints on her breath mixed together with cigarettes

and another odour, something adult and sour.
"'Alo Augusto," she said as I walked through the gate and up the path.

Lucho stood on his toes to kiss his mother good-bye. She offered him a cheek but gazed past him. As she turned, her gown gaped to show a pale sliver of breast that ricocheted guiltily around my head. I blushed. It reminded me of what I'd overheard my mother saying. That Ana-Maria had arrived in the town in a state of 'disgrace' and that Carlos was a lunatic and a Trotskyite spy.

Lucho and I left the yard and walked to school through a curtain of mist. I looked sidelong at him. His eyes were ruddy and bloodshot. His hat was still in place. I didn't want to talk about Paloma. He reached into his shorts and pulled out a marble. It was his "lucky special". A dollop of clear glass the size of an eyeball. It was shot through with twists of silver. Carlos had given it to him. He polished it on his shirt.

"What's a Trotskyite?" I asked.

He stowed the marble and rifled through his satchel. He pulled out a banana and peeled it, squinting at each stringy piece of skin.

"I think it's a bad person." he said.

"At least, the carabineros don't like them. Ana-Maria says that before I was born the carabineros took Carlos away one night 'cos they thought he was one. When they brought him back he wasn't right in the head. They said that he'd fallen down the stairs trying to escape. They took her away too. They did other things to her."

The school was a single-story prefabricated building with a flat metal roof. The heat of summer and the cold of winter had turned its walls into a patchwork of grey concrete and peeling yellow paint.

Each interior wall of the classrooms were decorated with portraits of winners of the Copper Company sweep-stake. The ruddy faces of winning breeders stared down from the walls. Each owner puffed out their chest and clutched their impassive prize bird.

Lucho's name produced a chorus of chicken noises, when attendance was called. The loudest clucks came from behind me, from Eduardo Gallo Junior. I looked round. A wad of chewed paper stung me between the eyes and plopped onto my desk.

Profesora Reyes kicked Gallo out of class. "Hijo de Puta!" he hissed as he passed by, tossing a piece of paper at Lucho.

Our first lesson of the day was Biology. This was my favourite lesson, ever since I'd been given an atlas of extinct animals for Christmas years before.

I used to take the book to bed with me and read it under the blankets with a torch. I'd run my tongue around the exotic names, sounding them out. I'd absorb the embossed pictures with my fingertips.

Eo-hip-pus: a horse the size of a dog. A-ep-yor-nis: a flightless bird the size of an elephant. Ars-in-othe-ri-um: a hoofed animal, like a rhinoceros, with horns that protruded from its nose like twin mountains of bone.

Lucho normally sat in science lessons soaking up each point. He'd write notes and draw diagrams with his tongue protruding from the corner of his mouth like a pink slug. Today though, he spent the lesson looking out of the window as though waiting for something.

At lunchtime, we played marbles. The clouds licked at the school roof and rolled down into the fields beyond. Lucho sniffed at the air and pulled down his hat. He lost the game but I let him keep his marble. It was his favourite, after all.

Profesora Reyes appeared in the yard and sounded a triangle to mark the start of afternoon classes. Lucho pulled out the paper Gallo had thrown at him and unfolded it. It showed a stick figure being snapped in half by a huge bird. It was drawn in the same red ink as the

note on Paloma's body.
Beneath the picture, it said:
"Dear lieing HIJO DE PUTA! Did you have a NICE weakend? YOU and ME today at 4 oclok. By the old roble tree in the PARK."
Lucho screwed the paper into a ball.
"Are you going?" I said.
He looked at me.
"What's the point?" he said.
*
After school, we took the long way home. We walked along a path of hard-packed, red earth littered with dried pine needles.
At its edge, the trees nestled in dense clusters. They were good for climbing in the summer and the best pine cones fell there in the autumn.
We played paratroopers. Lucho had watched the 'The Longest Day" on telly the previous Sunday. He had worn his rubber-soled plimsoles ever since, so that he could jump out of a tree and land with his feet wide apart.
He clambered up to where two thick branches split in a 'y' shape.
He readied himself to jump -
"Oye, birdboy!" Gallo bellowed, "I bet you thought you'd got away didn't you, you weedy little shit-head."
"You're a coward," he continued, "and my Dad says that you're a liar, a bastard and your mum is a filthy puta … a whore!"
Lucho looked down. He pushed his glasses up to hook them under his hat. He swallowed.
Gallo was large and heavy. He had a tree-trunk of a body and wore long trousers. His face was the colour and texture of a pork pie. Before moving to Paraíso, his father had worked in a mine in the interior as a boy. All of the family were heavyset with short legs, long muscular arms and fists like cannonballs.

"Fuck off! You fuckin' nitwit!" shouted Lucho.
I had never heard Lucho swear before.
Carmino Marquez, the tallest and dirtiest of Gallo's troupe materialised from behind one of the trees.
"What the fuck are you laughing at you fuckin' puto! Faggot!" he shouted at me and swung a potato-sized fist at my head. The blow struck my temple. Everything went purple. The next thing he was straddling my chest and pinning my arms over my head. Carmino hawked and let a long, dark spindle of drool drip towards my face.
"Get off him, you fucker!"
I didn't see Lucho jump but I felt the impact of his rubber shoes as they hit the dirt.
He rocketed towards Gallo, whistling like a steam engine and windmilling his arms as he smacked into him. Gallo, stunned by the ferocity of the attack, staggered. One of Lucho's whirling fists connected with Gallo's flat nose. There was a cracking sound and Gallo struck the ground. Lucho hopped onto Gallo's chest and levered a bony knee across one of his arms.
Gallo swung his free arm at Lucho's head. He missed.
Carmino and I watched.
Gallo wriggled beneath his opponent. Each time he tried to sit up Lucho thumped him to the ground. Gallo's face erupted into tears.
Lucho was crying too. A trail of snot and spit began a slow elastic journey from the tip of his nose towards Gallo's face. He punctuated each blow with a sobbed "Paloma".
"Your friend's a fuckin' loony!" said Carmino hopping off me and running away into the trees. The rest of Gallo's goon-squad followed.
I ran over and grabbed Lucho's thin wrists.
"Ya basta," I said, "that's enough now."
He emerged from his trance. Gallo lay unmoving beneath him. I got Lucho to his feet and together we walked back

to the path. We were both shaking from the fight. I brushed dirt and pine needles from his face.

I looked at him and gasped. At first, I thought that his hat had been coated in mud. Instead, I realised that it had been pushed back from his forehead. In place of his red hair were thick tufts the colour of ash.

Lucho looked at the ground.

"I tried to cut it," he said, pulling his hat back over his eyebrows," … but after … it came… all my hair went this colour."

We walked a few steps. He sniffled and rubbed his nose.

"What really happened?" I said.

We walked for minutes then he swallowed. He closed his eyes and shuddered.

"It was afternoon. I'd been out in the back. Ana-Maria asked me to hang out the washing."

He closed his eyes and smoothed the hat down on his head with both hands.

"Then I heard it. The flapping noise. At first I thought it was the sheets. But it was lower and slower."

"The sky went black and the wind stopped. The flapping got louder and then I smelt something. It was like when Taracena's puppy brought home that dead cat."

A cold gust stirred the pine needles on the path.

"And then something wonderful happened," he said.

"I was flying."

He looked at his hands.

"I saw my house, and the trees in your yard. Then Ana-Maria came running out, screaming and yelling and waving."

"'Don't worry,' I shouted, but I don't think she heard me 'cos she just kept yelling and screaming."

"Then I felt this pain in my shoulder. It was sharp and pinching and I thought it must be like in 'The Alamo' when John Wayne gets stabbed."

"And I tried looking up but all I could see was a black

cloud. The pain in my shoulder was getting worse and it felt like someone had put their fingers in my ears, but I wasn't frightened. I remember worrying that, Ana-Maria would be angry if I'd ruined my jumper."

He leant forward and started to draw spirals in the earth with his toe.

"Then there was a popping sound and my toes hurt like they'd been shut in a door. Then there was another pop and I went lower and lower."

He felt in his pocket and drew out a cigarette. It was one of the singles I bought from the almacén. The fight had bent it into an 'L' shape. He passed it to me and I broke off the stump and lit it.

"and then I heard 'Arre! Arre!' from the backyard and saw Carlos running around. He was waving his blunderbuss. Then I felt sick in my stomach and I was falling."

Lucho coughed as the smoke clutched his lungs. He looked green and tears filled his eyes.

"I don't remember much else. Ana-Maria says they found me in Saucedo's orchard at the foot of one of the almendros. There were nuts and leaves and feathers everywhere. He was furious."

He spluttered and passed me the cigarette. The clouds had cleared and the edge of the sky was purple.

"C'mon, we've got to get home," he said. "Your mum will be worrying."

*

The carabineros, the pacos, were waiting for us outside Lucho's house when we arrived. I discovered later that Carmino Marquez had told his mother that Lucho had murdered Gallo. She had phoned the police.

The pacos, one fat, one thin, leant against their patrol car in their green military uniforms. Their pistol grips and badges glinted red in the setting sun.

Lucho pulled a face and waved me back with a thin arm.

He raised a finger to his mouth.
Ana-Maria sat on the front-door step, her head in her hands. She looked pale and scared. Carlos stood guard in the yard midway between Ana-Maria and the police. A streak of bright blue light from the patrol car slid across the house. Lucho sank to his haunches. His face lined with worry. He sniffed and his eyes filled with water. He looked up at the sky.
"I can't cause more trouble," he said.
I wanted to hug him at that moment. I wanted to hug him and tell him not to worry. That it was all going to be all right. That things would work out.
There was a flicker of warm wind. He breathed in and stood up. He looked taller and older. He reached into his pocket and pulled out his marble.
"Here," he said, handing it to me, and then he tucked his glasses under the rim of his hat and sprinted across the yard.
The pacos spotted him as he was halfway across. They both ran full pelt towards him.
Ana-Maria's face lit up. She opened her arms wide.
"Stop them!" squealed Lucho. He ducked and slipped under her. His hat dangled in her hand. She turned and ran after him.
Hearing Lucho's words, Carlos launched himself at the fat paco.
"Hasta la victoria para siempre!" he shouted as they collided and rolled through the scrub. The paco's baton whipped into a bush. A few steps behind, the thin one leapt over his partner and into the doorway. I knew what I had to do.
The paco galloped up two or three stairs at a time. I reached the staircase and threw myself at his boot. I hugged the shiny leather and hung on.
The paco fell onto the stairs face-down with an "Oof!" He wriggled and kicked as though wiping something off of

his shoe. Above us, I heard Lucho's feet scramble for purchase on the metal roof. Ana-Maria screamed his name.

The paco swore and kicked at me again. I looked at his face. I pulled on his leg keeping him off balance. He worked himself upright and freed his truncheon. Lucho's voice echoed through the yard.

"Ahora! Ahora! Now! I'm here! Estoy Aqui!"

I shut my eyes and grimaced, gripping the paco's foot till my knuckles went white. And for the second time that day. Lucho saved me from a beating.

The paco and I both heard it. The low throated throb of something old and unimaginably heavy in motion. A sound so deep that you felt it rather than heard it. The paco's night-stick paused mid-strike. Then it came again. Higher this time and closer. A rumbling flap somewhere between low, distant thunder and the sound of the waves when a storm blew in from the sea.

"A-ha! Ya viene! Something's coming!" shouted Carlos.

The paco kicked free, jumped over me and ran out onto the front yard. I followed him, jumping the last few stairs and cannon-balling through the door. I stumbled over the step and fell into the dirt of the yard. Both pacos stood facing the roof. Carlos sat handcuffed to the wooden gate. His mouth smeared with blood.

"Here!" shouted Lucho.

I twisted round, but he wasn't talking to me. He stood on the roof with his back to us. His plimsoles slung over his neck. He straddled the corrugated metal and raised both his hands. The wind tousled his tufts of silver hair. Then behind him, I saw it.

An enormous velvet shape gliding in with the encroaching night. It blocked out the stars as it came, riding along the spur of the milky way. It swallowed stars with each flap of its wings. The trees in my back yard shuddered as the downdraft tore their leaves away.

“Thar she blows!” shouted Carlos, hopping up and down and laughing.

The monolithic winged-shape swooped down behind Lucho. It was the size of a plane. The size of a moon-rocket. Each colossal wing-beat brought it closer, driving a bow-wave of smells ahead of it.

Lucho was right. It did smell like the odour that Taracena’s dog had brought home with it, but that was only one of the smells. It was earthy. It carried the perfume of the rain and the trees and the mountains. Its aroma carried traces of the dark moonless nights before speech or thought or history. It was the smell of something older than man. Older than the world.

The pacos were rooted to the spot. Lucho stood on tiptoes, his grey hair standing on end. Each wing-beat felt like a blow and then there was a monumental rustling sound.

I couldn’t hear Carlos’s yelps of glee or Lucho’s incantations. But as I looked up, Lucho turned to face us and smiled. Behind him, Ana-Maria swung onto the roof clinging to its surface. She shuffled forwards. Lucho took two steps to the edge of roof, breathed in, and leapt off. Ana-Maria screamed and lunged after him. They fell into space.

For a second they hung there, suspended in the night and the sudden silence. And then something wonderful happened.

Lucho and Ana-Maria flew.

Lucho’s feet kicked and his arms stretched out beneath the wing-shaped eclipse that held them. Ana-Maria giggled. I had never heard her giggle.

I looked up with my mouth open. The creature’s plumage seemed to swallow the street-lights and pale blue pulse of the police car.

Its feathers were larger than my body. They were as black as coal and tipped with velvet. Its body was as long and dark as a whale and each wing was long enough to span the yard. I caught a glimpse of a glistening hooked beak and an eye like a black dinner plate.

They soared so low over the yard that Lucho's toes dragged parallel tracks in the dirt of the yard. He grabbed the thin paco's cap as he passed and then they swooped up, up and over the street. Carlos whooped as they passed over the Gallo's house. They turned back towards the cliffs and flew far out to sea. The pacos left without a word. The fat one had pissed himself.

*

Sometimes now, I go over to Carlos's and I help him with his rum rations. We sit on his roof and talk about Lucho and Ana-Maria. We talk about how Gallo recovered from his beating and how he never bullied anyone again. And then we sit and wonder if Lucho and his mother will come back.

"Maybe they never will," Carlos says, clacking his plates.

And sometimes on those evenings he'll sing a sea-shanty and I will take Lucho's marble out of the pocket that I keep it in and hold it to my eye and squint at the moon. And sometimes, if the light is right and the breeze is earthy and warm, I'll see a tiny boy dangling in the sky beneath a bird the size of plane. A bird so big that it eclipses the sun.

And I'll know, as much as I know anything, that he and Ana-Maria are happy and safe and glad to be gone from Paraíso.

If you believe that sort of thing, that is.

Philip Suggars

Grateful Lives

Her shift at Jefferson Elementary had finished, but instead of stepping out the side door to the playground and walking the five blocks home, Emma Kinder clocked out, bided some time in the women's restroom (the damp one the size of a closet, which other custodians called the spider pit), and after the children had all filed out to the diesel-spewing buses, leaving a smell of sticky milk and sour child-sweat in the hallways, she descended the stairs to the basement boiler room, where she would hide out until the principal was gone.

A bulb dangled over a wooden table. The table was knife-scratched and abandoned by the janitor who'd worked there before. The dim-yellow forty watts couldn't cast light up the stairs. It didn't matter. Nobody would notice her. Nobody, it seemed, ever did. Except of course for Ramsay. Her husband. He was the reason she wouldn't be going home.

The night before, Ramsay had returned from work at ten o'clock. He would have stayed out later, she knew, but he had lived in Jefferson Village long enough to know that even in the north, white towns weren't places to be getting drunk after midnight. Also, Emma knew, Ramsay would be anxious to return home. He'd be anxious to attend to her. That's how he put it. Attend to her.

Ramsay had lost his job. Since Emma was the one who paid the bills and balanced the checkbooks, she knew that, unless some pack of angels wired thousands into their joint account, they would miss yet another payment on the mortgage, and soon, inevitably, they would forfeit the house. It had been a long time coming, and even though Ramsay had never talked about it, she knew the rumors of impending lay-offs at the tool and die had transformed into more than anxious whispers and indignant diatribes at the local manor. For one thing, over these last weeks, the injuries she suffered had been getting worse—from fist-bruises on the hammy meat of her shoulder, to teeth indentations in her neck. But nothing could have prepared her for last night. While she'd been washing dishes, Ramsay had clamored up behind and heel-kicked her in the hip with one of his grease-smoothed leather boots. "You did this to me," he'd slurred. He'd held his hands up to his face as if some gash or burns tore across his skin. They lived in a one-story, three-room ranch out on Mills Road. No neighbors, if they'd heard, had bothered to call the cops. Ramsay had torn the work slacks down from her waist, his voice jagged and deep behind her, and dug his hands into the soft flab around her hips.

"That ripping," he'd said, his lips against her ear, "that ripping that's there is death." Then his hands were mashing her face into the linoleum kitchen floor. "That's all there is now. That's all that's coming next."

When Emma was a girl, she was the first of her family who'd come from Georgia to Ohio and gone to school. She was a cocoa-skinned, wiry girl among mostly freckled, floppy-haired farm kids. Sometimes when she thought back to it, she laughed: with her speed and powerful voice (you had to learn to move quickly, to shout like the devil was behind you, growing up with three older brothers), she must've overwhelmed the subdued, mechanical movements of hay-baling, tractor-driving kids. In spite of it all, in elementary school, she'd blended in as part of the sensual pungency of early, public school socialization, and everything from the milk-sticky cafeteria floors to the waxy crayon residue underneath fingernails—it all had belonged to her. Emma, back in the 1960s, was Jefferson Elementary School's rapid heart beat.

Maybe because she had never gone to high school, painful memories had never spoiled the ones she'd kept from

Jefferson El. And really aside from drive-by shouts of nigger from cars (shouts aimed at her family house down on East Elm, or aimed at her as she stepped from the convenience store or, once, from church), nobody in Jefferson was cruel. In the end, she thought, that was all anyone could really ask for. Yes. She knew the town's excessive politeness—opening doors for her when she went to the post office, or the burger girl with thick black eye shadow smiling and maintaining the polite grin and eye contact a little longer than was called for—reminded her she wasn't white. They were adults, after all. No more selfless exuberance or child-sweat jubilation on playgrounds.

Some hours later, when she was sure all the children had boarded the buses and were gone, Emma lifted her head from the table. The light bulb was flickering. It would soon die. She had drifted off and didn't know what time it was. A sour taste of sleep coated her mouth.
The flashing light threw a shadow on the cinderblock wall across from her. Rope, crusty with time and damp with basement mold, coiled down from a nail angled into a wooden support beam. She knew that rope, its fibers frayed and rough around her skin, wouldn't snap.
Before she could balance herself up from the chair, the light bulb slowly dimmed until it was a glowing worm of light. The ember persisted but eventually extinguished itself.

She felt her way to the stairs. The door to the basement could be locked from the outside. If she had slept too long, Mister Walter, the elementary school principal, might have walked past the boiler room, noticed the unlocked door, and thrown the bolt. The wooden railing was smooth in her hand as she scaled up. Boards wobbled and creaked under the weight of her steps. As she'd feared, the door was fastened closed, and no light slanted through. In case anyone was still in the building, she stopped at the top of the staircase and pushed her body against the door. She laid her hand around the brass knob but didn't turn it. Instead, she eased her ear against the wood, and listened.

She strained to catch any stray echo, of clacking shoes or Mister Walter's jangling keys. She couldn't be sure what time it was but guessed she'd slept until eight. That darkness oozing in around the door happened only after the sun had sunk behind the line of Jefferson's black oak woodlands it prided itself on. The best deer and wild turkey hunting in Ashtabula County, some said. Just last year, a stray bullet from some hunter's rifle had ricocheted crooked off a tree in those woods and hurtled through the wall of their lawnmower shed out back. Ramsay had gone out to the shed and stood in there for a long time. He'd poked his finger through the bullet's entry point. A jagged edge had ripped through the pad of one finger. That night in bed, he'd said that he'd been unable to hunt down the place where the mangled bullet had buried itself. He hadn't slept. He'd gone out at night with a flashlight and come back smelling of bitter soil: he'd been digging. In his imagination, the lost round that had probably been meant for a turkey or deer or coyote may as well have been a land mine.

That hidden damage, some quiet vitiation, penetrated both their lives, and Emma knew that, if she were to go home now, Ramsay would be the one to explode. He might not kill her, or mean to kill her, but he would attack, and that ripping pain was something she would not be going home to.

Emma pushed on the door. It was locked. She tightened her jaw, with the blackness of the yawning basement behind her (the shadow of the rope coil, its anodyne roughness, was still etched in her eyes), and bumped it with her shoulder. The latch jiggled. Mister Walter must've thrown it closed during his final check of the building before going home.

Pressed up against the door, she lifted her face toward the blackened, spider-webbed ceiling and shut her eyes.

She'd be locked down here all night. Maybe she could use this as an excuse—if Ramsay asked—but Ramsay-from-before was dead, and after last night, she was sure there'd be no more sentimental making up, followed by sometimes weeks of relative peace, before his fist shattered her jaw or knocked the breath out of her. No, she wasn't going home as long as she was alive. Her resolve, though, didn't erase the feeling she would have when someone, maybe Mister Walter, found out she'd been locked in the basement all night. She murmured a plea to the absent shadow of the boiler basement, closed her eyes, and laid her forehead against the surface of the door.

The sound that reverberated through the wood, of metal clicking and grinding as the door latch opened, was icy water over her shoulders.

She knew what she'd heard, and all at once she knew what had happened (the door had opened), but she paused for a moment, knowing at the same time that it couldn't be true. The door swung open to ash-gray student lockers, no taller than child caskets, and the swirling darkness of the hallway.

The decades old, outdated public-announcement system, with its dials and sliding buttons, hulked against the wall in Mister Walter's office. On top stood a silver microphone, a fat shiny ribbon mike that reminded Emma of the ones all the blues and rock singers once clasped in ecstasy as if pulling girls in to kiss. Each morning, Mister Walter stood here and made morning announcements.

Streetlights along Elm Street glowed in blurry globes outside. The light seeped into fabric night shadows. The only sheriff cruiser in Ashtabula County, the one the county could afford after budget cuts, coasted by, slow, the officer leaning forward over the wheel to check on the building. Emma froze. She waited for the cop to glimpse her as she stood there in the principal's office. Maybe Ramsay had reported her missing. She'd be arrested, maybe even charged with something like trespassing, but the cruiser rolled on. Once again, nobody had noticed her. While she was standing there, an electric hum of white noise crackled from the speakers of the PA system.

At first she thought she'd bumped something, switched over some dial. She watched the machine. The sound from the two round, screened speakers flickered. She neared it and leaned over. No lights glowed to indicate how she'd accidentally turned the thing on.

She opened her mouth to mutter a self-admonishing, "Oh, Emma," and her voice crashed down around her from wall-mounted speakers. It echoed down the hall—Oh, Emma, emma, emma—reverberating, she knew, through every room of the empty school, echoing down the hallways that, during the day, she swept, mopped, and scraped free of bubble gum. "It's open," she said, meaning the microphone, but her voice must've missed the mike that time. Instead of booming through the school, those words perished on her lips.

Her voice quieted around her. It evaporated outward, its final tremor pulsating in some upstairs corner. She was alone with herself again, divided, a person in a dark room who nobody, even police officers trained to notice, could see, while the sound of her escaped voice lingered. It persisted somewhere, past the sweet-smelling wooden floorboards of the auditorium stage, through the narrow staircases and lime-green painted walls. Somewhere in the far rooms of the school, past rows of smudged, miniature spider-harboring lockers, a wisp of that echo still stirred. The thought of following it made her shiver. Mister

Walter had flipped off all the lights. She'd have to grope blindly through the corridors.

The machine in front of her, if she pushed buttons, could monitor those rooms. She'd seen teachers do it before, come to speak with Mister Walter and, almost as an experiment, listen in on their students. A kid would shush the rest of them, the nervous boy whose parents had instilled anxiety and competition, but crayon scribblings and long division were eventually pushed aside and the kids would flap open an umbrella of noise, a kind of stratosphere multiplying some central childhood impulse.

I'm no teacher, Emma thought, but she reached a finger and pushed the button to what she thought was an upstairs room. Crackling returned through the speakers. She stabbed her finger into the button again to shut it off.

She opened her eyes, wide, and looked around the room—at Mister Walter's family photos, his son and daughter smudged out in the night, the corners of books and papers, a stapler, hole-puncher, and paper-cutter on the counter where parents, when they came, sometimes rested their arms. If her mother could see her now, she thought.

Her mother, who'd ridden that Greyhound in 1953 from that plot of chocolate-rich soil and stones in Morbin, Georgia, to the station in Ashtabula City, stomach cushioning Emma inside. Her mother, who'd worked twenty-nine years sweeping coal dust off hundreds of yards of docks and sidewalk in Ashtabula Harbor. Who'd died of stomach cancer that devoured through to her kidneys, liver, and outer-lining of the heart, and who'd walked with Emma, every morning, down blocks of Jefferson Village to the elementary school, because she loved her daughter too much to shoulder away that shield between Emma and the rest of the town.

Emma raised another finger, and as she pushed the button a second time, she closed her eyes and felt her mother's tough-tendon fingers squeeze.

The noise from before crackled through the speakers.

Emma withdrew her hand and hugged herself. She tilted her head toward the machine's speakers. It was time to go home, whether she liked it or not. The classrooms were empty. All of them.

What came next through the PA system's speakers, though she thought she'd turned the thing off, were murmurings at first. Emma held still, straining to hear. She leaned closer, then jerked back.

"No," she said. "It can't be." It was almost the sound of children's laughter.

It's open, she thought. Oh, Emma.

She stood, unable to move in the growing noise. It was impossible, but still she heard them. The children's voices gathered. The sound peaked into crashing jubilation, then changed.

It distorted through the speakers. Emma backed away.

It should be beautiful. Not like this.

She tore away from the room and ran out the door. Her shoes squeaked over the waxed floor tiles, and the blinding swirl of the hallways spread like smoke around her. The children's lockers blurred by on both sides.

The room that beckoned was on the second floor, at the end of the hall. A balloon lifted and bounced from the door. She walked closer.

It was a party. They'd been waiting. A girl ran forward and clasped Emma's hands and pulled her in. The light in the room was orange but grainy. It would lighten up. She knew it would. There were cookies to eat, red punch to sip from paper cups.

It’s your party, Emma, and it was the voice of her mother. And it was true. Emma’s name sagged across the chalkboard. It hung from a string noosed around paper letters snipped free by children’s hands.

justin nicholes

"Sometimes, not all the time," he said. "But sometimes I wonder..."
"What do you wonder?"
"What I'd look like if I was fat," he said, pulling the passenger-side mirror down and gazing at himself. Often I've thought of Kelly as different, borderline troubled–like he's got some social disorder from being knocked around too much as a kid. And I almost said it out-loud but I refrained due to his constant convicted expressions. Instead, I only sighed and nodded. I ran my hands down the wheel and held it at "eight" and "five", right above my crotch. If he weren't in the car with me, one of my hands would be in there, scratching away. I shifted uncomfortably and tried not to hate his presence.
"Sometimes I wonder what kind of donut I'd be," I said, feeding the flame of his stupidity.
"Yeah, me too," he said thoughtfully. "I'd be a cinnamon sugar twist. The best kind."
"Cool," I said.
I also wondered what my life would have been like if I didn't listen to my parents, went to a trade school instead (like I wanted to), and never went to college. I went for graphic design when everyone and their cat were applying, too. I went right at the time that they were hiring like mad for the position and by the time I came out, bright-eyed and innocent, the market shit the bed and there were nothing but dead-end jobs in my hometown and already filled positions in the city. This dead-end job is how I met Kelly, a skinny idiot from the sticks. I was from the sticks too, but we were a heterogeneous bunch, never easy to pinpoint, always surprising. You'd never think your pizza delivery boy had a Bachelor's in Fine Arts, was on the Dean's List all four years and had a strange knack for fixing toilets. That was my real interest:

plumbing and maintenance. My doctor father turned his nose up at this. My lawyer mother talked me out of it. Kelly, well, he was never sure what he wanted to be outside of a donut. I'm not sure ambition was something he was capable of. I had been training him in the art of pizza delivery for a week and he still didn't know how to deal with money or people. The only reason he wasn't fired was that his older brother owned the place.

He had some talents. He really knew his way around places. You could drive him to the middle of nowhere, blind-fold him, spin him around and punch him in the balls and he'd know which way was home. He was like a homing pigeon, same brains too. He'd be fine as a delivery guy except the last time we left him alone he took two slices of pizza for himself because they didn't give him a tip. While they stood there, handing over the money, he politely opened the pizza box and took two pieces, leaving them dumbstruck as he made his way down their porch. He wasn't malicious or anything; he just thought it was right and deserved. I couldn't help but love him a little for it.

In the five days I'd driven Kelly around, I learned that his favorite television show was still the Ninja Turtles cartoon from the nineties, his favorite band was Nickelback and his favorite female was Jessica Alba. I think his love for Nickelback was only because his brother liked it. Jessica Alba and the Turtles was his own thing; I was pretty sure of that.

My phone vibrated in my pants. It was my mother calling me. I ignored it and slipped it back into my pocket.

"Who was that?" Kelly asked.

"Your mom," I said. "I left my boxers in her bedroom."

Kelly said nothing for a long moment and then, everything clicked into place. He gave me a side-glance, smiled and punched me in the arm.

"You're a real dick sock," he said.

"Dick sock?" I asked, intrigued.

"Yeah," he said, licking his lips. "It's the thing you put your dick in to jerk off with. That's you. You're an old, used up dick sock."

"Thanks," I said, laughing.

There would be total, unbridled depression floating in the interior of my rasping 2001 Taurus if it weren't for the job in Manhattan. Every day I lived in a quiet, unfocused anticipation for this distant but possible promise of a better life.

Their name was Peripheral Design Group, but I didn't let their marginal company title discourage me. I applied, hoping for an interview, and a week later I got a call. I had a thirty-minute phone interview that went really well, but they didn't welcome me down to New York for something in-person. They said they'd call me by Friday if they were interested. It was already Wednesday. I checked my phone like a text-hungry tween. I must have driven Kelly a little nuts from it.

Whatever happened, whatever Kelly said or didn't do right to mess up another delivery, it was all okay because I felt–I mean, I truly believed–that there was something on the horizon. I was young, on the stale side of twenty-one, and ready for whatever life had for me.

We pulled in to two-sixteen Charter Lane. The car crunched over loose gravel and came to a tired halt before the front door. It was a typical house: a dumb whirly-gig in the yard, a house-shaped mailbox, flowers everywhere, plastic siding over old wood–a Colonial with a face-lift. I knew this place. I used to ride by it on my bike.

We stepped out of the car; Kelly went first like an energetic, police K-9. He carefully carried the pizza in its usual red delivery bag. We walked up to the door together as I put on my cap that read: "Astro Pizza: Out of This World". After Kelly's older brother Ted ordered the hats, he discovered the "h" was missing on all of them. Instead of complaining or mailing them all back (things that took effort), he just sat Kelly down with a black sharpie and a bag of Doritos and told him to take care of it.

Kelly rang the doorbell. I could feel the energy emanating from him, the anticipation. I watched him there at the front porch, standing beside me with his mouth half-open, his skinny shoulders slumped over, and envied the bastard. I wished I could be this ridiculously happy over something so simple and stupid. I hated him for it, but only a little, and only for a moment.

The door opened to reveal a curvy, thirty-something woman in a bathrobe. She had her hair down and a glass of wine in her hand. She must have just gotten out of the shower. I imagined what she was like under that robe, and felt myself start to stand at attention.

"Hi! Astro Pizza!" Kelly the genius said. I softened immediately.

"Jason?" she asked, her head tilted.

"Yeah, that's me."

"Oh my god, I'm Janet."

"I'm Kelly."

As if he wasn't there, she looked at me and smiled. "Do you remember me?"

"Not really, no," I said, shrugging.

"I was your babysitter. For like, a whole summer. You were a little monster."

"Oh my god, Jan?"

"Yeah!"

"You look great!"

"So do you!"

"Nah."

"No, you do. Take the stupid hat off." I did. "Look at that dark hair. And you're all filled out, look at you. You look…you look good, Jason."

"I'm Kelly."

We looked at Kelly. Crickets chirped.

"Hi, Kelly," Janet said.
"Your pizza's gonna be ten bucks."
"Okay," Janet said, and dug into the pockets of her robe. She gave me a funny look and I cringed, apologizing for Kelly's abrupt personality. "It takes two guys to deliver pizza?"
"I'm training him," I said.
She handed over the ten with a few dollars on top. Kelly saw this and smiled, enthusiastically handing the pizza over to her.
"You should stop by sometime," she said. The box pressed against the thin fabric of her robe, pulling the collar open a little further. I didn't stare, but Kelly did.
"Yeah, I will," I said.
"Cool."
"See ya," Kelly said. Janet gave me one more up and down look before closing the door. I felt like a piece of meat and I loved it. Women my age around here were unappreciative. At least the ones I ran into.
As we got back into my car, I wondered if Janet would be turned off if I told her I had crabs. The answer was obvious but I was hopeful anyway. Realistically, I knew it would have to wait until they cleared up to make any visits like that.
"She was hot," Kelly said, throwing his seat belt over his chest and clicking the buckle.
"Let me ask you something," I said. "Let's say she didn't tip you. What would you have done?"
"Thrown her pizza in the woods."
I looked at him for a long moment. He smiled.
"No, stupid, I'd a just said, 'have a nice night'."
"Okay," I said, turning the key in the ignition. "Just making sure."
#
"How's he doing?" Ted asked. He threw a pizza in the oven and said, "Hector, watch this. I'm getting a smoke."

Then Ted jerked his neck toward the back door and I followed him out.

I put an arm on the dumpster as he moved the cinderblock in front of the door to keep it open. Ted was tall, muscular, nothing like his brother. He was a good-looking guy, too. It's almost like everything good went to Ted, except most of the time he was kind of an ass-hole. He was more like an Eddy than a Ted.

"He did okay today."

"Just okay?" he asked, lighting a Camel.

"He's just…he's a little abrupt."

"Abrupt?" The cigarette bounced between his lips.

"Well, yeah, like…he's just a little short with people. You know, if they don't pay the second the door's opened. Stuff like that."

"So it's his personality now?"

"Yeah," I said.

"It don't take personality to deliver pizza."

I laughed. "I think it takes a little, Ted."

Ted put his hands on his hips and shrugged. He looked over across the street at the little blue building that used to be a video store before Netflix happened. "Cock" was scrawled over the front window in graffiti.

"I don't know what to do about him," he said distantly. It was the most pensive he'd ever been around me. I felt kind of special that he chose to share his doubts with me, like I was an advisor to him.

"Maybe he should go back to cleaning."

"He hates that, Jason," he said. "He's twenty-four, he doesn't want to clean the rest of his life. And no one else would ever hire him."

"So…I continue training?"

"Yup," he said.

"Until what?"

"Until he gets it."

You can't just teach a person to have personality. It was

an impossible task, and something I was going to ignore and let work itself out. It wasn't my responsibility to undo years of social inadequacies. Some people are delivery guys and some people clean the floors. And some people are big-time graphic designers in Manhattan with a nice car, proud parents and no crabs to speak of. That's just the way it goes.

#

The next morning I sat at my computer with Peripheral's website up. I absently brushed my teeth with one hand while scrolling through the About Us section with the other. This was about the tenth time I read it over.

"Jason?"

I turned, my toothbrush dropping from my mouth. My mom stood in the doorway with a cup of steaming coffee in her hand. She wore a polo shirt and light-colored shorts. It meant that she and my dad were going out to play golf soon.

I grabbed my toothbrush off the floor and popped it back in and continued brushing.

"Yeah?"

"First off all, it's ten o'clock, why aren't you dressed?"

"I'm getting there."

"Second, don't brush your teeth at the computer. That's a terrible habit your father started you on and I want it to stop. Third, Peripheral called-"

I bolted out of my chair and almost knocked her over running down the hall to the landline when she shouted, "Kidding!"

I stopped. I hated her. Without a word to her, I turned and went into the bathroom and finished brushing my teeth, my heart sinking in my chest. She did this shit to me all the time.

"I'm sorry," she said. "I was playing around."

"Not funny."

"I know." She sipped her coffee and watched me for a

moment.
"What?"
"Let's say you don't get this."
"Great."
"Well, what are you going to do?"
"Die," I said.
"Okay, drama queen."
"Mom, it's important."
"I know it is, but…what I'm trying to say is that if you don't get it, have you considered moving down there anyway? Getting your own place and networking? Maybe getting an entry-level design job somewhere?"
"Move out?"
"Yeah."
"Are you telling me or asking me?"
She sighed, "I'm telling you, honey. I'll even pay the rent for the first three months."
I put the toothbrush in the holder and rested my hands on the sink basin.
"I'm not even sure if that's what I want, Mom."
"Don't tell me that. A hundred thousand dollars later, please don't tell me a thing like that. I don't want to go back to heavy drugs."
I gave her a look.
"Kidding," she said.
"I did college for you," I said. "I did a good job. And now you're kicking me out?"
"You're twenty-two."
"Twenty-one."
"Right," she said. "Jason, you need to live on your own. I don't care if it's down the street or in Sri Lanka, you have to make it on your own."
"I feel like…"
"What?"
"You're throwing me to the wolves."
"How else are you going to grow up?" she said. "You

want to end up like that slow kid you drive around? Kelly?"
"He's different, don't compare me to him."
"He's no different. He was coddled his whole life. Did you know that he's a math genius?"
"No," I said.
"He could be at MIT right now, or in a great job somewhere but he's not because he's babied. So toughen up and get out there. You're twenty-one years old for god's sake."
She walked away, worked up but feeling good about herself. I punched the porcelain sink with the meaty side of my hand and started the shower. I made it hot enough that it hurt.
#
I put the pizza on the counter and went to find Kelly. We had a fifteen-minute window of time to deliver, and even though Kelly could do no wrong, I could. I didn't want Ted up my ass because Kelly made me late.
I found them in the back room with the dirty dishes. Kelly absently picked at a dirty pie tray, his shoulders slumped, his head down and nodding. Ted stood, his arms crossed, his muscles straining under his NIN t-shirt. He was trying to get Kelly to look at him.
I stayed by the door and put my hands in my pockets. I checked my phone: nothing. It was six-thirty on a Friday night and their office closed at seven. I bit my lip and focused on Ted and Kelly, trying not to think about Peripheral.
"Will you just look at me?" Ted said, putting a hand on his shoulder. Kelly looked at him. "I think you're great. Jason likes riding around with you." Ted glanced at me and back at Kelly.
"He does?"
"Of course. All I need from you is to let Jason do the talking for a little while. Just listen to him. Learn from

him. You can do that."
"Sure," he said.
"Good."
I cleared my throat and Kelly turned. The pie sheet he was picking dropped off the rack and onto the floor. It sounded much worse than it was. After Kelly put the tray back, I said, "We got a delivery."
We drove down one fifty-three toward Rupert onto Blossom Road. It was well beyond the fifteen minutes because I had to get gas and Kelly must have taken the longest pee in recorded history. Still, when you're the only pizza place within twenty miles, it's hard to find real complainers.
We pulled into a small nook in the forest. Set back in a semi-circle of pine trees was a white, rusted trailer. A sedan, much like mine, sat in the driveway beside a new Dodge pickup. A rusted swing set loomed motionless in the yard. We stood at the doorway with the pizza, warm in my hands. There was a television murmuring from within. Kelly knocked on the front door. It made a rattling noise.
It opened. On the other side stood a tiny toothless girl with blonde pigtails and a pink dress.
"It's my birthday!" she said, jumping up and down. "Daddy! Pizza! Daddy!"
A tall, thin man in glasses appeared behind her. She grabbed his thigh and rested her head on him as he went through his wallet.
"Sorry about her, she's a little nutty tonight."
"Don't worry about it," I said. "How old are you?"
"Five!"
"How exciting!" I said, handing the pizza over. Kelly stood beside me like a stiff board, lips pressed together, arms to his sides. He stared straight ahead, expressionless. The dad noticed this, adjusted his glasses and asked how much he owed.

"Ten," I said kindly.

He handed the money to me: a five and a ten.

"Thanks, guys," he said.

"Thank you. Have a good night. Happy birthday, Princess!"

As the door shut, I heard the little girl say, "Daddy, he called me a Princess!"

"I know he did," the dad said.

Kelly was silent as we made our way down the winding road back to one fifty-three.

"What's wrong, man?" I asked.

"I don't want to do this anymore," he said. I was surprised to hear it. I thought he had found his calling in life.

"Why's that?"

"Ted said I can't talk to people."

"I think he just meant for you to listen a little more. Listen to how I do it."

"But I'd say the same stuff you say!"

"But…"

"But what?"

"You're kind of forceful. Your tone is forceful. A little demanding. For the cash I mean."

"I don't know what you're talking about."

"I'm sorry, but it is," I said. "And it's almost worse now because when you stand there saying nothing, just staring straight ahead you creep people out!"

Kelly punched the armrest under the window, hard. I was surprised by his strength. He put a hand over his mouth and looked out the window, watching the trees fly by. Streaks of sunlight illuminated the car at our backs.

"Hey, you want me to put on EQX?" I asked, reaching for the dial. It was a station we both agreed on, found common ground with.

"Fuck it," he said through his hand. I let my hand drop, snuck a quick nut scratch and wished I were somewhere else.

#

Twenty minutes later we were on the road again. Kelly had a couple words with Ted and seemed to feel a little better. He was smiling stupidly again, like normal. He had one foot up on the dashboard and EQX was playing. The windows were down; the summer air was blowing a crosswind through the car.

I checked my phone. It was eight-thirty. In that moment, it became clear to me: I didn't get the job. It felt as if someone put their foot on my heart and stomped.

"Who do you like better: Ghana or Germany?"

"I don't know, Kelly."

"I like Germany. Hector likes Ghana. We both think France sucks."

"Mm-hm."

"Who you think's gonna win?"

I shrugged.

"The squid thing says it's gonna be Germany, Hector thinks Spain's gonna take it."

"It's an octopus."

"It's a squid."

"No, it's not. It's called Paul the fucking octopus, so it's a goddamn octopus."

"Hector calls it a squid."

"Hector can't speak English!"

"Well, I think it's a squid, I'm pretty sure of that," Kelly said. "I'll ask Ted when we get back, he'll know."

"Kelly, I'm telling you what it is. It's a motherfucking octopus called Paul and this is an asinine conversation anyway so shut the hell up." I shut off EQX. We sat in silence for a long time as I went too fast down route twenty-nine.

"You can be a real dick," Kelly said.

I pulled the car over. Kelly sat upright, bracing himself. I got out, walked down to the ditch and into an alfalfa field. I screamed. I screamed, letting out my murderous, raging boredom and utter disappointment until I couldn't scream anymore. It felt good.

I went back to the car, turned on the radio and continued down the road. Kelly just looked at me, bewildered.

"I like Ireland's team," I said.

"They didn't play."

"I know."

#

We pulled into the driveway of a three-story white house. It was a Victorian, but not the trashy, neglected kind. They always reminded me of dusty, rich old women. Of tragedy. This Victorian was well maintained, with groomed shrubs out front and a new paint-job. It could have been a bed and breakfast.

"Ted said I could talk," Kelly told me as we walked up the lawn to the front porch.

"Fine with me," I said. Kelly rang the doorbell.

We waited.

He rang it again a few minutes later. Finally, the door opened. On the other side was Chris Valencia, the biggest asshole in town. This kid used to pants me in junior high, invite me to hang out with him and his friends and send me on errands the whole night, he'd push me into lockers, flip my food tray, read off my tests in class–the usual bullshit.

He used to be bigger than me, but I caught up. I hadn't seen him since graduation day and I hoped I'd never see him again. His blonde hair was shaved down to his skull; he wore a tight gray shirt and shorts. He was in good shape, always was. I wondered if he was still an asshole. Mainly, I hoped he wouldn't recognize me. I wanted him to think I was off doing better things in life, that I'd "made it".

"Holy shit," he said. He recognized me all right. "Jason? Jason Stone?"

"Yeah," I said.

"Ho-lee Shit."
"Hey, Chris."
"How are you, man?"
"Okay, you?"
"Chilling," he said. "This what you're doing now?"
"For now," I said. "I got a job lined up in New York for the fall. Design company."
"No way," he said.
"You do?" Kelly asked. "I thought you said you wanted to go full time in the fall?"
Chris smiled at Kelly and then at me.
"No," I said. "I got that job."
"That's great, Jason!" Kelly said.
I felt terrible about the lie but I didn't know what else to do. I knew Chris wanted to see me fail and I wasn't going to give it to him.
I asked Chris, "What are you doing now?"
"For now? Just helping my dad. Learning about construction."
"Awesome," I said, hardly masking my envy.
"I just ran five miles so I need some serious grease."
"I hear you," I said, smiling. It wasn't a genuine smile but I don't think Chris cared. I hated running, never understood it.
I handed over the pizza and the check. Chris disappeared behind the half-closed door for a moment and came back with a fat, brown wallet. I heard Kelly's wet mouth fall open a little. I wanted to punch him.
Chris pulled out a ten and two ones from a fat stack of twenties and fifties. He handed the money to me. He gave me exactly what he owed us, with no tip. Chris put his wallet away and I heard Kelly swallow. He was pissed.
"See you, Chris," I said, and turned. I was halfway down the steps with Kelly when I heard: "Jason?"
I turned back. My throat went dry, the hair on the back of my neck stood up, my balls itched worse than ever. It was

she: Stephanie, the bitch who gave me crabs.
"Hi," I said. She was dressed for sex: a black tank with a push-up bra, tight jeans and high-heel boots. She looked nice, sexy, even. When we got down to business the first and only time, we were both so drunk that I don't remember much about it. Only the after-effects. She looked this nice the night we did it, before she worked her magic on me and cursed me like an old gypsy.
Chris put a proud arm around her.
"You know each other?" he asked.
"A little," I said.
"I just saw Chris at the track today."
"My Uncle's got a racehorse there," he added.
"Haven't seen him since high school."
"Doing some catching up?" I asked.
"Something like that," Chris said, smiling.
"Aw," Kelly said. "I gotta piss. Can I use your bathroom, man?"
I shook my head at Kelly. Chris grinned and said, "No, you can use the side of Jason's car, though." Stephanie giggled. I put my hands on my hips like Ted and gave him a wry smile, like I didn't care.
"Oh, I can't do that," Kelly said, frowning. "You'd hate that, right Jason?"
Chris laughed harder. "Who is this guy?"
"I'm Kelly," he said.
"He's like a skinny Costello. You know, like from Abbott and Costello?"
"What's that?" Kelly asked.
"You should watch it, it's uncanny."
"Chris." I said. To Kelly I said, "Let's go."
"Can't believe this is our lives," Chris said. "Years later, here I am living the dream and you're," he laughed, "also living the dream."
"I wouldn't say that," I said.
"Your dream isn't delivering pizzas and driving retards

around?"
Kelly was at him before I could blink. He was skinny, weak, but fast. He had Chris by the collar; the pizza had fallen from Chris's hands to the porch floor. Stephanie had her hand over her mouth and Chris was laughing. I pulled Kelly off of him, directed him down the steps to the car and told him to go sit inside. He flipped Chris the bird and did what I said.

Stephanie was bent over, closing the pizza box up. Her breasts almost popped out from the top of her tank.

I tore my eyes from her and looked at Chris, who fixed his shirt.

"I'm sorry about him," I said.

"I was just playing around," he grinned.

"I really am leaving in the fall," I said.

"So if I order pizza you better not show up here," he said. After a moment he said thoughtfully, "No one wants to be here forever."

"Not even you?"

"No way, I hate it here. Boring as hell."

That made me feel a little better. I appreciated the ass-hole's honesty. I guess he owed it to me for calling my friend a retard. Kelly got that a lot in school and we all knew it was a soft spot for him.

"I'll go get us plates," Stephanie said. "Nice to see you, Jason." She walked away, her heels clicking and her ass swinging back and forth until she was gone.

"Damn," Chris said, looking after her. "Hey, did you and her eh…did you do her?"

"No," I said. "She's just a friend. I don't think she's interested in me."

"Really?" he said. "She'd probably consider it. Hey, I'll let you know how it goes."

"Yeah," I said, smiling. "Have fun."

"Tell Kelly to toughen up," he said. "I was kidding."

"Sure," I said. Chris shut the door.

I got in the car and started the engine. I caught Kelly wiping a tear off his cheek. He stared out the window, silent.

"He wanted me to tell you that he was sorry," I said.

"Yeah, right, Jason."

I drove off. I heard his breath hitch once and then he seemed to be over it. The guy was too sensitive for the world, for other people. I couldn't understand why he didn't want to stick to cleaning. All he had to deal with was a few grease stains, some muddy floors. Leave the jackasses and the dumb bitches to people like Ted and me.

"Why do you do this to yourself?" I asked, as I pulled into the parking lot.

"I didn't do anything."

"No, I mean you know this is hard. Why do you insist on doing it? My mom said you could go to MIT if you wanted."

"Because, Jason," he said. "I'm afraid of people."

"Really?"

"Yeah," he said. "All they want is something other than what they have. And it makes me nervous. If all I do is clean, I'll never get over this. And if I don't get over it, I'm just going to be a total fuck up to Ted. And he's going to hate me forever for it."

"Ted doesn't hate you."

"Yeah, he does." Kelly stared at his palms.

"If it counts for anything, I don't think you're a retard."

"Oh, I know I'm not either," Kelly said, laughing. "I was just pissed that I didn't punch the bastard."

Whether I believed Kelly or not, it didn't really matter. Regardless, I wanted to clear something up with him.

"I didn't get that design job."

"You didn't?"

"No," I said.

"Then why'd you say you did?"

“Because I didn’t want that dick to think that this job was all I had.”
“What’s wrong with this job?” Kelly asked, a little hurt.
“Nothing,” I said. “I’m just…”
“You should stop worrying what other people think of you. Especially dick socks like him.”
“Yeah,” I said. “You’re right.”
“Common sense,” Kelly shrugged.
In ten minutes we were back on the road to Lake Lauderdale with ten large pizzas steaming in the backseat. I took my phone out of my pants pocket and turned it off. It felt good to be unleashed from it. Like I was cut off from the world, a cowboy, or the lone ranger. Delivering pizzas like the Pony Express delivered mail.
Kelly put his foot up on the dashboard. Nirvana came on and it felt like I was a little kid again when I didn’t understand the lyrics but still liked the music. The pines opened up on Route twenty-two and I could see the lake shimmering in the night. Beds of algae floated at the top, beach house lights shined on the other side. To my right, The Burger Den was hopping. It was beautiful.

Elizabeth Green

"Did you see that?" Arnold asked. Ida, busy with the map, was trying to find out where in the hell they were. Somewhere in northern Indiana, that much at least was certain. Lost on a road that stubbornly defied identifying itself.

"See what, dear?" she said absently.

"That sign we just passed."

"No. I was busy trying to find us on the map. Did you see a road sign?"

"No. There was a sign outside that last cabin we past." Arnold was already slowing down and looking for a place to turn around. "I'm going back. At the very least we can ask them directions." Arnold found a logging road and managed to make a 3-point turn without getting them stuck in a ditch.

Ida folded the useless map and asked, "What did the sign say?"

"Here it comes, read it for yourself." The hand lettered sign sat beside the weedy drive. It read "Alien Artifacts" in six-inch high letters. That's all it said. Two words that held the promise of great wonder and mystery. How could anyone pass up a sign like that?

"Oh come on, Arnold. It has to be some kind of joke."

"Who puts up a joke sign in the middle of nowhere? Even if it is a joke, I bet the guy knows where we are and can help us get back to the Interstate."

Ida saw the logic in this argument. They had been lost all day, one wrong turn leading to another. Deeper and deeper into a maze of back roads. That sign was the first bit of civilization they'd seen in more than an hour.

The driveway was little more than two streaks of bare earth leading into the scrub. They bumped and scraped along for about a mile until a house and barn appeared before them. Another hand lettered sign said parking.

There were no other cars. The house was dilapidated and weather-beaten to a uniform dull gray. The barn was in the same depressed condition. A large faded sign over the barn indicated the entrance to the exhibit.

"Come on, Ida, I think it's open."

"I don't like the looks of this place, Arnold, I think we ought to leave."

"Oh come on, Ida, don't be a stick in the mud. This could be fun"

"I thought you said we would get directions."

"We will, honey, just as soon as we find somebody to ask."

Ida shook her head. It was useless arguing with Arnold when his mind was made up. Indeed, Arnold was already out of the car and walking up to the barn. He turned and motioned Ida to follow. Afraid of being left alone, she reluctantly joined him on the path.

Arnold peeked inside the dim barn. There was a small collection box by the door that said admission was free but donations were gratefully accepted. Arnold stuffed in a ten-dollar bill in the slot and he and Ida entered the barn. As soon as they cleared the threshold the overhead lights blinked a few times then stayed on.

The first exhibit was a poster sized aerial photograph of an empty field. The sign said that the field was the crash site of an extra-terrestrial spacecraft that plowed to the earth and burned on August 23rd 1956 on the old Henderson Farm. There was a copy of a faded newspaper article showing an eager young Henderson shaking hands with an Air Force General. The headline read, "Military examines mystery object." The caption under the photo said, "Air Force General William C. Bankhurst congratulates Inwood, Indiana, resident, Hiram Henderson on his amazing find."

"I guess we're in Inwood, Indiana," said Arnold. "See, this stop's already paying off."

"Great, can we go now?" Ida didn't like the feel of the place.
"A few more minutes. Lets look at the wreckage."
The barn was divided into aisles with tables filled with charred hunks of twisted metal, which signs proclaimed were pieces of the craft's fuselage. The salvaged pieces looked for all the world like rusted car parts and melted Tupperware containers. One table contained a jumble of bits and pieces the sign said were the remains of the cockpit, the highlight of which was a half melted computer keyboard with weird symbols in place of the familiar alphabet. A sign claimed that the keyboard was proof of the alien's advanced technology as there were no Earthly computers in 1956.
"Pretty hokey," Arnold stage whispered to Ida.
"It all looks so fake," Ida whispered back.
The next table was filled with what the sign claimed was "The Crew's Personal Effects" the centerpiece of which was a spacesuit which looked very much like a ratty old wet suit and scuba tanks paired up with a WW II Army Surplus gas mask. When Arnold saw it he burst out laughing. The sign said that the tanks contained an unbreathable mixture of methane and helium and was proof that the aliens did indeed come from another world. Also on the table was an item that looked like a television remote painted green and funny symbols applied to the keys. A few dented and burnt tuna fish cans identified as rations concluded the exhibit.
The last object before the exit was a large glass cylinder labeled "Alien Transporter Booth, Take your picture inside."
"That would make a perfect souvenir. Ida, you have the camera?" Arnold opened the door to the enclosure and stepped inside. Ida fished around in her bag for the digital camera she always carried. When she looked up to snap the photo, Arnold was gone. The air smelled faintly of

ozone and the cylinder door was closed.
"Arnold, this is not funny," Ida looked under the tables expecting to see him hiding there. When he didn't show up, she began to panic. "Arnold. Arnold." She called and ran from the barn. She ran to the house and pounded on the front door. It dawned on her how silent and alone they had been the whole time never seeing another person. She pounded on the door with more urgency. No one answered so she tried the knob. To her surprise, the door opened upon a rather conventional looking living room with old-fashioned furniture on a faded oriental rug.
"Hello. Is anyone home?" Ida stepped into the room. "Anyone? I need help." She heard a sound at the back of the house where she expected the kitchen was. "Hello? Can someone help me?" She didn't notice the door had closed behind her. The last thing she did notice was several tall figures wearing what looked like ratty old wet suits topped with World War Two era gas masks. As they advanced on her she fainted.
Several space-suited aliens carried Ida upstairs and laid her on a gurney where she was probed and examined with a series of curious instruments. When they were finished with Ida, they did similar things to Arnold.
Some hours later, they came to their senses. They were back in their car at a rest stop fifty miles North of Inwood. Both had only vague memories of what happened and disturbing dreams for years after but at least they knew where they were.

Harris Tobias

The Wreck of the Margaret La Salle

What's a man gotta do for a drink around here
The stranger banged his fist on the bar
The bartender poured him a shot and a beer
Before the stranger could take it too far

Now listen my friends and I'll tell you a tale
Of passion and pathos and pain
About how the good ship Margaret la Salle
Went down with all hands in the rain

Three points to starboard the old captain wailed
We're heading into a blow
Batten the hatches and reef all the sails
We're taking on water below

There's rocks on the port side there's rocks all around
Cried the lookout up on the mast
Steer hard to starboard or we'll certainly be drowned
And we'll all soon be breathing our last

The mate turned the wheel and the ship came about
Just missing the rocks to the East
But it wasn't the same for the rocks in the South
They grinned like your old granny's teeth

The rest of the bar was now crowded around
To hear of the crew's dreadful plight
They refilled his glass and made not a sound
As he told of that harrowing night

A wave picked us up and smashed us back down
With such force that our lookout was flung
All the way back to his house in the town
And there on his weather vane hung

But the storm wasn't through with the Margaret la Salle
She had plenty more tricks up her sleeve
The captain ordered us into the boats
But we were too frightened to leave

Get into those boats he yelled to the crew
Or you'll nere see yer loved ones again
But that was something we just couldn't do
And we stayed on the deck in the rain

The captain and ten of his most trusting men
Separated themselves from the crew
We assume that they came to a terrible end
For they soon disappeared from our view

Here the stranger paused with his hand on his heart
For the death of the captain and men
Then he drank down his beer and took up his part
And plunged in to his story again

There were only three of us left on the deck
The cook and the bosun and me
Then the ship and the rocks made a terrible wreck
And all of us drowned in the sea

Now wait just a minute the assembly cried
You're not dead, you're standing right here
You think that I don't know when I died
And he fixed us in place with a sneer

Then his image wavered and faded and dimmed
Until we couldn't believe what we saw
Just a place at the bar where the stranger had been
And a funny wet spot on the floor

For there on the floor was a puddle of beer
Still steaming and foamy and warm

In the shape of a sailor, eyes widened with fear
Floating and drowned in a storm

I'm a sailor myself and I know what I know
And I've heard many a marvelous tale
But I never heard of as dreadful a blow
As the wreck of the Margaret la Salle

Harris Tobias

Nancy

It was nearly Christmas when Lori's grandchildren, both in their twenties, arrived with a gift. Lori, my neighbor across the street, had spent the better part of a decade as a widow and she lived definitively alone inside her fading yellow house. It was this solitude that inspired the present.

I was tending my roses when the girls raucously emptied out of their tiny red Volkswagen—they could not have been bubblier. One of the girls had tied a pink ribbon around the animal's neck. All of their excitement and joy was met, on the cement slab that was Lori's front porch, with an equal and opposing force of disapproval.

"Fine, we understand, you don't want her. We just thought it might be nice for you to have a friend, that's all."

"Well, I thank you for your intentions, but I don't need the extra burden of caring for an animal."

The girls had expected this resistance.

"Could you just watch her for a few days, until we get back?" asked the brunette.

"We're going to Aunt Pauline's," said the blonde, "She doesn't allow pets."

"Well, girls, you should have thought about all this beforehand. If you would have thought to call first, I would have told you no over the phone, and saved you the trouble of buying a…" Lori paused to recall the breed.

"Staffordshire Bull Terrier!" reminded both granddaughters in unison.

"Right, a dog, and transporting it two hundred miles!"

"We're sorry! It's only for three days and she's already potty-trained," said the younger, more persuasive blonde-haired grandchild.

"Fine, I'll watch her, but you really should have better thought this through, girls."

"We're sorry. This is her food and this is her leash. She's had all her shots so if you want to take her for a walk, feel free."
"And we haven't named her yet so call her anything."

If the girls had chosen to do so, they would have been the first visitors to go inside their grandmother's yellow house in several years. The car's engine never stopped running and they were gone in twelve minutes, just enough time to leave a dog and a bag of supplies.
Lori took the animal inside and I didn't see them again until that evening—she took the dog once around the block. The couple walked unhurriedly, calmly, as if they had done the walk a million times before and would do the walk a million times again.
Early the following morning, Lori left the house again. This time, the tiny dog was wearing a hand-knit purple sweater, presumably to combat the mildly cold weather. Lori was wearing a purple jumpsuit of the same fabric. I was already outside in the garden that morning; it was the first time I heard the dog's name. They crossed the street in royal fashion: Lori held the leash high in her left hand so as to encourage the dog's head to be upright and alert. They trotted proudly across the street, as if competing at the Westminster Dog Show. Lori was only eighty three then.
"Hello Beth, I want you to meet a little friend of mine. This is Nancy."
I had not seen Lori smile in a decade and would soon get used to seeing her perfect false teeth. The red Volkswagen came back late the following day, but, of course, the girls left without Nancy.

For the next fifteen years the two walked twice a day, three loops in the morning and three loops at dusk. I never asked why they chose to walk counterclockwise during the evening hour, I assume it was to better see the sun set. Lori must have knitted twenty or more sweaters for that dog. On most days, the color of their garments matched almost to perfection. They were in love from day one. Lori became an expert on the breed, eventually competing in dog shows. I cut out a photo of Lori and Nancy, from the newspaper, after they won a statewide event.

"Well, it's Nancy that does all the work. I just have to hold the leash and try to keep up," Lori would say laughingly.

Although the dog stayed relatively short, its small frame packed on gratuitous muscle. The animal's head was disproportionately large in comparison to its body. After researching Staffordshire Bull Terriers at the library, and discovering how the breed was once used for bull baiting in England, I no longer allowed my grandson, Alex, to play with Nancy.

One day, without forewarning, Lori brought a puppy home, a pug I believe. The following morning Lori didn't take either dog for a walk, nor did she endeavor outside that evening. The next day was the same, a silent yellow house. I figured Lori was busy trying to train her new puppy. It is my opinion that the new dog was meant to learn the finer qualities of a dog, from Nancy, before she died. However, after not seeing Lori leave the house for an entire week, my concern grew. I crossed the street carrying a can of pepper spray in my purse. When Lori failed to answer the door, I turned the knob and admitted myself. Immediately both dogs mobbed me with licks.

"Lori, are you home?" There was no answer. The house smelled of scented candles and dog feces. The kitchen was empty, except for several poops spiraled neatly atop the linoleum floor. The living room was vacant and the hallway was still. The door to the master bedroom was cracked open and I peered inside. There, tucked snugly under the blankets, lay Lori. I stood in the doorway and watched her tiny body—she was not breathing. I walked over to her bed and stared down, expecting to see the pacified face of an elderly woman who had passed to death painlessly in her sleep. This was not the face I saw. Her eyes, though grayed and lifeless, still beamed with terror. Her mouth, half agape, was silently screaming. Upon grabbing the sheet, in order to cover the head, I felt an unsettling texture—the linens had been soaked in blood and dried to an unnaturally stiffened state. Small red holes confirmed that Lori's neck had been clamped shut by the mouth of a Staffordshire Bull Terrier.

Dustin Hyman

Brandon Tires

A young man of twenty-two sits on a black bench seat that once rested inside a 1971 Ford racing car. He waits impatiently in blue jeans and a white T-shirt for his mechanic to give him the 'okay' head nod. This will indicate that whatever problem his car had, it's been resolved, and to please come up to the counter in order to square away the bill. Not having much money, the young man always calls three or more mechanics when a problem with his vehicle surfaces. More often than not, if he can do the work, Brandon is the cheapest bidder. Today the young man has no money to pay Brandon. Brandon's office is bigger than most. The floor is covered with black and white linoleum tiles. Directly in front of the register, heavy foot traffic has scuffed the white tiles dark. The young man sits between a magazine rack and a tall dusty houseplant. A short empty desk near the register holds piles of yellow, white and pink papers. A large, stern but friendly woman once sat there. She had big black hair nested atop a round white face. She wore red lipstick. The young man used to know Brandon's wife Delores very well. She was kind and direct because she had to be.

The phone on her desk rings now—once, twice, "Brandon Tires," declares Brandon. On the phone, he discusses part particulars for a transmission while searching for information on an outdated computer.

"Ya, we can get it, gonna be about two weeks, though." Brandon squints hard through old lenses to double check the writing on the screen. He stands inside an oil-stained denim jacket with the large black phone pressed firmly against his sagging ear.

"Oh, so ya don't need it…gonna find it online?" Brandon pauses to hear justifications before relaying a long list of numbers from the dingy screen. With a confused, if not angry expression, Brandon hangs up the phone. He takes a moment to look through the big windows of his shop's face before walking towards a side door that leads into the garage. Brandon stops to get water from the tank beside the door. He flips the valve open and liquid burps into a cone shaped paper cup. Brandon gulps down the water and opens the door—a loud scream from a power tool zooms past him as he enters the noisy garage. The young man is alone in the office now. He grows agitated and restless on the warm leather bench.

Two minutes pass before the bells above the store's entrance ring out a warning. A weathered man of about forty years walks in wearing a black ten-gallon hat. He nods towards the seated man and approaches the counter. The younger man nods back but the cowboy has already looked away. He is not tall but walks as if he were a giant. At the counter, he pats calloused hands onto the hard clear plastic that covers the wood. The cowboy leans over the tall counter to better see through the side door's square window. He then walks over and peers through the smudged glass. Satisfied, he enters. The laughter of two men can be heard on a.m. radio until the door slams shut. The young man gets up from the bench and stalks toward the side door. He takes one glimpse through the window before creeping back to the bench. A minute later, Brandon tows the cowboy back into the office. The boy in blue jeans pretends not to notice them reenter the room.

"How ya getting along?" the man asks Brandon.

"Truth be told, Leroy, it's been pretty rough. Delores was a good woman. Things were easier when she was taking calls." Brandon says this vacantly and then stares down expectantly.

"I hope it's not too soon to ask this, Brandon, but are you gonna see any money for your loss?"

"Well, it is too soon, but since you thought it important enough to ask—yes. I'll be getting some money from

insurance. Fairly soon I hope."
"I meant no offense, Brandon, just makin' sure you're gonna be alright, that's all." Leroy checks the bench behind him before continuing in a library voice, "You know I loved her. I loved her as much as you did, Brandon." The two men suffer in silence.
"So?" With raised eyebrows Brandon progresses the conversation, "whada ya want, Leroy?"
"Well, it's not me actually—my son. You've seen Corey's truck, he's got that big-old lift on it." Brandon concedes by closing his eyes and then nodding disapprovingly.
"Well, I told em' if he raised some money, I'd go half in on some big-old knobby tires, so that his truck don't look so pussy." The man smiles, trying to make friendly, but Brandon's white mustache remains flat across his face, until he asks, "About how big you wanna go with these things?" Leroy thinks for a moment.
"How much for a set of BFG's—36×30's?"
Brandon bends down to search the computer, "Be about $650," he says before rising to face Leroy again.
"Jesus, Brando, I was thinkin' more like $540." Leroy looks down and gently taps his work-boot against the exhausted floor.
"Kid might just have ta' save a bit longer," he eventually announces with a grin. Brandon thinks on the matter. He looks at the computer, then at the register, and then back to the tiny cowboy, who is waiting patiently under the black brim of his hat for negotiations.
"I can give ya 10% markdown, Leroy."
"Well, all the same, I better go let him know how much they are and see what he wants ta do." Leroy taps the counter again, "Ya know, my neighbor Tucker said Wal-Mart actually has a decent selection on rubber."
"They do. That's why they can afford to sell em so cheap—they order so God-damn many." Brandon's voice

is no longer apathetic, “I’ll tell ya right now, they’ll be about eighty bucks cheaper at Wal-Mart.”

“That much, huh? Well, all the same, I’ll go ask the kid what he thinks and we’ll let ya know.” Leroy shakes Brandon’s hand and turns to leave. The young man in the white shirt hastily flips pages with damp fingers, pretending to read words from a Field and Stream magazine. Halfway to the exit, Leroy stops. He acknowledges the seated young man with another nod before returning to the counter and Brandon.

“Ya know, Brandon, I gotta be frank with ya, and because ya don’t have much time I’m just gonna say this.” He continues in the library voice, “Ya know I got a C.B. radio in the Chevy. I usually keep it tuned to the police frequency, so I know what’s going on in town, and so I can help in case of an emergency—been first on scene twice.” Leroy is whispering now. He leans over the counter to be more near Brandon’s tired ear. “Well, after Sal gets done with an accident on highway 41 he’s got orders from Sheriff Carson to drag your ass in.”

“Me? What they want me for?”

“Well, they found something strange in the autopsy report—found poison in Delores’ blood. Usually, when someone jumps off Becket’s Bridge, they know the end is comin’. Poison or no poison.”

“Well, it’s not my fault if Delores was a thorough woman is it? Does that make me criminal?”

“God no, they just found it strange and was wondering if you knew anything about it—thought they oughta let ya know is all. I just wanted ta give ya the heads up. Give you some time ta prepare.”

Both men stand up tall and peer around the office. The young man keeps turning pages—he knows better than to stare at two grown men whispering.

“Ya know, Brandon. I been hearing some things in town. Some crazy shit.”

"Oh ya? Ya gonna tell me what ya heard Leroy or make me guess?"
Leroy leans close again, "I heard Delores was fuckin' some punk kid that plays ball for Butte College."
Brandon stands tall and looks down at the little cowboy. "Get the fuck out of here Leroy."
Leroy backs away from the counter and then turns to exit. "Tell your boy, Brandon's closed!" he shouts as tiny bells sound Leroy's exit. Brandon walks over to the side door, turns the greasy brass knob, and enters into the garage, slamming the door behind him.
The young man stands to look outside; Leroy is making a phone call inside his blue Chevy. After turning from the window and approaching the front desk, the young man eyes the register and then steals a glimpse through the side door's small window. He picks up a tall trophy from the counter and turns it upside down—he swings it through the air as if it were a baseball bat. The trophy is crowned with a golden race-car. A small copper plaque is mounted onto the trophy's heavy marble base. It reads:
-1st Place-
-Santa Maria Speed-Way-
-1972-
"This will do," he mumbles to himself before gently setting the trophy down in the same exact spot—the rectangle without dust. The young man walks over to the small desk beside the counter and opens the top drawer. He reaches inside and grabs a blue scarf that had belonged to Delores. After giving the fabric one long smell he replaces it inside the drawer. He walks cautiously back to his seat near the ficus crying.
Brandon reenters the office a short while later with a shiny chrome pistol tucked between his belt and his back. He nods 'okay' to the seated man in blue jeans before tossing him the car's keys. The young man catches the keys and then stands to meet with Brandon at the register.

He eyes the tall trophy and then looks at Brandon. Outside, a black and white police car skids to a stop beside Leroy's Chevrolet. Sal exits the vehicle and approaches the shop with his gun drawn. Leroy follows Sal inside Brandon Tires with a deer rifle. Shots ring out. A minute later bells jingle and the young man walks outside. His white-T shirt is stained red and he's carrying Brandon's gold trophy in one hand, the other hand is clenching Delores' blue scarf.

Dustin Hyman

On the Road of Black Thread

The shadows split,
like her gown,
in the darkness
surrounding her tomb.
Where she walks
on iron circles.
Waiting
for his eyes
to break her
like stone.

A.J. Huffman

Shivering like a Pinned Butterfly

She can’t hide in this desert.
It’s too bright.
Though she tries.
Curling tighter and tighter,
every morning,
against the wind.
But the sun never fails
to find her.
Of course, it isn’t hard.
It simply follows the bloody footprints
that lead
to her tired rainbow’s end.

A.J. Huffman

Harvest Season

The stretch of the yellow
rice fields rustles within
the scythe's arc.

Air funnels between
the blades. The grass
breathes; it will die soon.

Kristine Ong Muslim

Small Town Cats

When the cats found the tuft of grass lining
the border, they crossed it to get to the city.

On their first few nights in the city, they could not sleep.
The lights were never turned off. The siren sounds
of ambulances and police cars went on and on.
Dead bodies were dumped on the alleys,
where they rested their paws
and licked their small-town fur clean.
The city people howled all day and fought all night,
gambled by midmorning and killed themselves by noon.
How every thing moved:
the children poked at their whiskers,
the homeless kicked them against the walls,
and the street gang leaders ripped their ears
to pledge allegiance to the fold.

One year later, their claws grated against the glass.
They made enough noise to wake the sleeping
small town people to let them in. At the end
of the day, their bowls were filled with fresh milk.

Kristine Ong Muslim

Small Town Chickens

The worms underneath
have burrowed deeply
years ago, leaving nothing
for scavenging chicken limbs.

Still they traipse on dirt to disclose
a trail of hieroglyphics.
Chicken feet are meant
to rake chicken circles
onto anything they touch.

They carve farewell messages
then ride toward their big town
dreams. In truckloads,
they come back featherless,
clucking back to their maternal hens.

Kristine Ong Muslim

A Small Town

It takes its name
from all the other caches
of meaningless names.

There will be cows and grass,
small town pulpits and a Sunday Mass,
small town dirt roads ending in doors
that lock in from the inside all memories.

There will be small town festivals
with colorful banners, parades
of decorated deities, clichéd
metronomic speeches of mayors
and cigar-smelling governors
and grinning mouse-faced vice mayors.

There will be gnarled and angry trees
along the side of the streets,
small town bums playing billiards
in fluorescent-lit rooms,
small town karaoke bars
barking in between
the silences of howling dogs,
and small town yards
with all the flowers
of the universe.

There will be ducks and chickens traipsing
their scrawls, languages, riddles upon dirt
and clothes and sheets flapping under the sun.

There will be hills and mountains seen from afar,
all kinds of fences for all kinds of trespassing feet,
rice and corn fields–their pained beauty like deliverance,

faucets that leak and eyes that seek
what lies beyond this small town wasteland.

There will be horses, sometimes white, sometimes not
that can not take anyone far enough
from small town incest and pedophiles and illegal loggers:
a regular small town merchandise.

There will be the ones who will quit,
the ones who will die,
the ones who will get pregnant in their teens,
the ones who will go to college,
the ones who will be killed,
and the ones who are not supposed to die.

There will be small town people
who will take care of their families,
send their kids to school, not beat the dogs
with their tainted feet or pass out drunk
in the middle of the street, and sometimes
tweak the ancient television antenna,
hoping to catch the face of God
behind the static.

Kristine Ong Muslim

The Small Town Project

This time, I want to get the song right,
but the sound dies back a few steps at a time.
Arriving in the city, I tell my story,
reciprocate the small town people
with memory:

Small town basketball players–
their agile bodies move:
so many branches, so many leaves,
so many years left to break them all.

Outside the house is the giant corn effigy;
it is ugly and grand. Carved on its base
are the names of small town people.
Population: 970. Established: 1877.
There is only one with a Ph.D.,
and there have been rumors
about that person's doctored curriculum vitae
while applying for university grants.

Makeshift television antennas protrude,
like sickly gods; they have been tweaked
by small town hands. Inside the houses,
the people crumble fruitcake with their hands.

All the small town people wake up early.
All the dirt roads end in doorsteps.
All the concrete roads begin
where all the welcome signs
tell every trespasser to leave.

Kristine Ong Muslim

The Death of Alia Rahman

Date: Monday, October 17th, 2020

Bleu sat in her classroom, and waited for her teacher to come, like the other students. She waited patiently, fixing the front of the class with her unwavering stare of glass. Every other girl in the classroom was talking, wondering how it is that their Professor would be late.

Bleu started to wonder that herself. This teacher had never been absent, never been late, in the five years that she has frequented this school. Especially given Miss Rahman's disciplined personality and temper, this was quite an event.

Miss Rahman was the one chiding students when they were late. She was the one lecturing students about responsibility, discipline, dignity, self-control. Respect. She was the one teaching little girls how to behave. Her being late was as inconceivable as Christmas in July.

And yet, thirty minutes passed without her crossing that class entrance. "Where is Miss Rahman?", yelled one girl.

"Is she absent? Couldn't she have picked another day?", inquired another.

Bleu had to listen to those kinds of comments for the past thirty minutes. Some of her classmates were being impatient, but some others, like her, were genuinely concerned.

Everybody held their breath as the door to the classroom opened, and someone stepped in, but not whom they were expecting. It was a man. And by the look of the white robe he wore atop his black suit and tie, a magistrate.

He paused after opening the door, and slowly walked towards the front desk, cutting through the heavy silence that plagued the room. He turned towards the student, and undertook the heavy task of delivering news that would forever alter their lives.

"Miss Rahman will not be coming to class. She has been found dead on the floor of her apartment late last night."

The news struck the entire class like a knife twisting through a wound. Bleu looked at the magistrate with an unwavering stare, and although she was profoundly troubled by these news, managed to keep her calm. Other students were not so fortunate.

* * *

The limp corpse of Miss Rahman lied on the floor of her apartment entrance hall, the red colour of dry blood having stained her white blouse near her heart, her legs folded under her grey skirt, her glasses broken in two, her hands lying on the ground, near her appalled face. Her black hair was completely undone, as if she had gone through some ordeal. She was surrounded with coroners and police officers, her entire room being scrutinized to find evidence.

* * *

"It would seem she was dealt a fatal blow to the heart with some sort of... weapon", the magistrate went on, despite the tears and protests of some girls in the classroom. "It was a murder. That is all we know for now."

He waited for everyone in the classroom to deal with their emotions in their own way, and leaned his back against the desk behind him.

"Your class is adjourned. The school is closed for the day. Her funeral will be held at the beginning of November, at a date we have yet to precise. We invite the entire school to assist."

Bleu kept on looking at the magistrate with her cold gaze, showing indifference, betraying profound sadness.

* * *

Arch-magistrate Elrun was standing in his office, eyes looking past his glass window to the far distances, hands behind his back. Two spheres of pure white energy floated around him, at a short distance from his body, in a fast and erratic fashion.

The door to his office was opened, and a light blue robed woman entered the room. She walked and stopped in front of the arch-magistrate's desk, bowed slightly, then went on to explain the reason of her presence.

"The other magistrates are quite worried about this situation, and we're all wondering what our response should be", said the female magistrate in a low-pitched voice. "Who could have done this?", the woman asked.

The arch-magistrate did not answer for a few moments, keeping his silence, looking through the window. "There has been a series of murders like this one for some time now, in a few cities. Berlin, Paris, Geneva, Monaco. The killings are not simultaneous, they happen one city at a time, one victim at a time."

He remained silent still, the two white spheres continued their fast and erratic way around his body.

"All victims were killed in the same fashion. One strike with some sort of blade, to the heart. This is the work of one man. Some renegade with a vendetta towards magic users."

Magistrate Airin took a step forward, visibly annoyed. "Why? Where can we find him?"

"I do not know his identity, and his motives are unclear", Arch-magistrate Elrun replied, still looking through his window, never turning around to face Mrs. Airin. "He acts in the shadows, he knows how to conceal himself. He targets all who are not pure humans".

Magistrate Airin was surprised, and a bit amused. "He wishes to fight the four races of magic users?" She sneered. "What a fool."

"At that he is", Elrun agreed. "But he killed a Professor of this school. If I ever encounter him, I will make him regret his actions. However, for now, we can only put our students and staff under surveillance, and wait. In time, we will uncover his identity, and his motives will be made clear. If he ever attacks one of us again, we will interfere."

He then went on to conclude: "However, should he attack other magic users who are not part of this School… May God have mercy on their souls."

Airin anticipated her superior's thoughts. "You have an idea who he is, though."

"Yes", he replied with his old yet powerful voice, still looking out the window of his office. With this answer, Airin waited for the man to elaborate, and, seeing as this conversation was seemingly over, she bowed slightly, and showed herself out, closing the door behind her. Another magistrate, a young male this time, with short brown hair and a black robe on top of his dark gray suit and tie, was waiting for her outside the office.

"So?", he asked.

Airin did not answer, but rather frowned.

* * *

Yusuke's father took a sip of his cup of coffee, sitting at the kitchen table across from his son and guest. Yusuke bore a serious look, while Orchid looked a little distraught.

"And this man did not attack you, you say?", he asked. Yusuke nodded positively.

The sky outside the house, as could be seen looking out the windows, was red, as the sun was setting.

They returned home after the announcement that their school was closed, and had been pretty silent ever since.

"But he might be the one that killed that Professor of yours", the father said while looking at them. Yusuke nodded again.

"I heard about a serial killer like that… This isn't the first murder executed in this fashion this year in Tokyo. It's just the first one you guys heard about, since it was so close to home. It seems unlikely these murders will stop, even if you don't hear about them."

"What did you say to him?", the father asked, drinking his coffee.

"Nothing. I was scared."

The father put his cup of coffee on the table and looked at his son with a bit of shame. And surprise. But mostly shame.

“You were scared?”, he said in a clear and reproachful tone. Neither Yusuke nor Orchid, sitting one close to the other, answered. “You have been taught how to defend yourself since you were a child, and you were scared?”, the father continued in the same clear and reproachful tone. “Why am I even bothering to keep her here, I might as well pack her bags and send her back to Tanaka.”

“No!”, both Yusuke and Orchid shouted with emotion, although Yusuke later wondered why he had objected with such vigor.

“I love my daddy…”, Orchid started. “But I love you too, uncle!And Yusuke as well!”, she yelled, not noticing how loud her voice was. Her eyes moistened. “I made friends here, Gwen, Hitomi… I don’t want to go back!”

Her voice broke with emotion. She found refuge in Yusuke’s chest, who surrounded her with his arms. Her tears lightly wet his shirt. Yusuke’s father remained silent for a while, pensive, drinking the rest of his coffee.

“I’ll call the school’s magistrates tomorrow and ask them what they intend to do about this…”

* * *

The days passed by, the leaves kept on falling, and the trees became barer every day. The atmosphere in the School of Magic was gloomy. Everyone tried to live their lives normally, but something in their heart was missing. Those who knew Miss Rahman were robbed of a powerful role model. The others, like Orchid, sulked in their dislike of death.

“Tell me, do you wish to protect his girl?”

“If so, you will need to be a lot stronger than you currently are. Otherwise, you will just end up dying. And so will she.”

These phrases haunted Yusuke like a refrain as he practiced his art on a punching bag, suspended in the middle of the training hall of his house. He kicked and punched until his fists bled, until his muscles were sore. Orchid stood up from the door of her room and watched the scene, with compassion, understanding, worry, and the lack of courage to interfere.

* * *

Date: Monday, November 1st, 2020

The trees were no longer a sight to behold. The grass froze under the chilling winds of the winter that was forthcoming, burnt from lack of maintenance. The students of the School of Magic and the School of Arts were gathered in a cemetery to witness the last moments of Miss Rahman’s unburied corpse.

They were gathered around her tomb, listening to a magistrate as he prayed for her safety, wherever she was headed. All were solemn, and those who knew her personally, and revered her like a second mother, were grievous.

Orchid, wearing a black dress, as was her new habit during a sad moment, took refuge in Yusuke’s chest, but did not cry. She was sad, but today, too strong to cry.

With final words of the magistrate, Miss Rahman’s tomb was buried into the ground, and all kept in their hearts the words of those who spoke respectfully of her life’s accomplishments as they headed back home. And all vowed to honour, during the remainder of their lifetime, the truths she had tried to instill her students in her teachings. Discipline. Dignity. Respect.

Fact sheet: Alia Rahman

Characteristics:
Academic specializations: Magic channeling practicum, rhetoric and languages
Date of birth: 4th of November 1981
Blood type: A
Hair style: Long black hair, often tied. Height: 150 lbs
Weight: 5′5 ft

About Alia Rahman:

Miss Rahman used to teach magic channeling practicum in the 7th and 8th grades, and rhetoric and languages in the 9th grade. She is a very strict teacher, and tries to discipline the young girls frequenting the Orchid School of Magic so they may grow to become dignified young ladies. She does not tolerate lateness, incompetence, or impudence, and punishes harshly those who make those offenses. However, she does not punish for the sake of punishing, but for the young girls to learn how to behave in the world, and knows when to reward her students with compassion and recognition.

A Sunni Arab born in Saudi Arabia, she studied and taught at King Saud University in Riyadh. She then became a Professor for the Japanese Orchid School of Magic, a job she loved, and never regretted taking on.

She is unmarried, and has no children. She made vows to a man, however. Her family, and would-be husband, had she survived, remained back in Saudi Arabia, where she returned during her summer vacations.

Alia is an Arabic name which bears the meaning of exalted, of the highest social standing.

Gary Germeil

Star-Crossed

Date: Wednesday, December 1st, 2020

The chants of birds no longer graced Japan. Light snowflakes fell gently from the sky to cover the ground with white. Orchid innocently tried to catch the snowflakes with her pinkish cloth mitts as she walked on the side of the street, looking at the white snow that gathered in her hands with the sparkling eyes of wonder and curiosity. Hers was about the first time she could remember the snow being this beautiful.

She had long forgotten anything else than her studies these past few weeks. This outing with her friends during lunch was more than welcome. She walked amidst Gwen and Hitomi as they walked on the sidewalk away from school.

She rubbed her mitts together as the soft winter breeze caressed her beautiful skin, and as she felt snowflakes land on her red hair. The fabric of her pink coat rubbed against itself and made some noise. She looked up, closed her eyes, and smiled as the snowflakes landed on her face. She then opened her eyes to look at the street covered in white, and comment on her appreciation of the phenomenon.

"It's so pretty…", she said with some awe and admiration in her voice.

"Is this your first time?", Gwen asked her, looking at her younger friend with a bit of amusement. Her long blond hair, some of it attached with a hair-slide, flowed with the gentle breeze. "It's like you've never witnessed winter before".

Orchid did not answer, conscious that whatever she witnessed in the past was never this majestic. Then, for a few seconds, she remembered her father's smile, and wondered what the winter snow looked like back home. Hitomi rubbed her green mitts against Orchid's winter jacket leave and looked at her suddenly quiet friend, concerned.

"What's wrong?", the dark brown haired Japanese girl asked Orchid.

"I miss my daddy…", Orchid said in a soft, wounded voice. Hitomi moaned as to appease her, and rested her short dark brown hair against Orchid's shoulder. The three remained silent as they walked on the side of the street.

It was Gwen who broke the silence, a little irritated. "Don't we all".

"I'm sorry…", Orchid said, not realizing that Gwen's parents were still back in Britain. She was living with her aunt and uncle in Japan. She rose her gaze towards her older friend, and smiled shyly. Gwen looked at her, then smiled back.

"Don't be sorry for me, I'll be seeing them soon."

Orchid was reassured by these words. She remembered. Gwen was in her final year at this school. Once the finals were over, she could then move back to Britain with her parents, and go to University.

"What do you plan to do afterwards?", she had once asked her tall, slender, older blond friend.

"Life isn't over after this School of Magic", Gwen once answered. "I can use my powers of healing and become a nurse, even a doctor. Understanding of magic to heal wounds, and understanding of the human body, this is an appropriate combination, don't you think?'

Gwen looked at her red-haired friend. Orchid had shortened her usual long hair a bit at a hair stylist, a few days back.

"What do you plan to do after you graduate?", she asked Orchid.

The red-haired maiden looked down, a bit ashamed about the fact that she had never thought about it. "I don't know…"

"I want to become a scholar!", Hitomi shouted in her high-pitched voice. Orchid looked at her. "A… scholar?"

Gwen looked at Hitomi too, with a dubious stare. "Yeah, a scholar?"

"This school was founded with the main purpose of studying magic, wasn't it? Where it comes from, what are its possibilities, how it interacts with the natural sciences, with the humanities, with the divine", Hitomi continued in the same breath.

Gwen looked upright, still a little dubious. "I guess you still have a year to think about it before you graduate…"

They stopped at a red light before crossing the street, and watched as numerous cars passed right in front of them.

"I'm serious Gwen, this is really something I'm excited about!", Hitomi said with a smile.

"You do know you need really high grades before you can even think about becoming a scholar in the School of Magic, right?"

Hitomi rubbed the back of her hair with a mitt and smiled, a little embarrassed about her very modest grades. As they waited, a gust of wind picked up, and Orchid had to hold her light gray skirt down with her hands in order for the wind not to reveal too much, much to her embarrassment, and much to the amusement of her two friends, who shared a common laughter.

Moments later, after the light turned green, they were inside a small coffee shop, sitting around a table, hot chocolate cups in front of them, Gwen's treat. Gwen benefited from discounts at this shop, since this is where she works part-time, after school, to pay for her personal expenses. She doesn't have the money to afford luxuries, but can indulge herself, and her friends, from time to time.

"So?", Hitomi asked Orchid, looking at her with a grin. Orchid seemingly wondered what kind of question that was, so Hitomi continued. "Have you met anyone in the school in front of ours that you like?", she said with a humorous tone. Orchid still had no clue as to what she was talking about.

Gwen drank from her cup, and tried to quench her thirst for gossip. "Any boy?", she asked. "We see you all the time with this guy, Yusuke you say his name was? Do you love him?", Gwen continued. Orchid blushed because of the pressure she felt her friends put on her shoulders, as they waited for an answer, silent and very interested, their bodies leaning towards Orchid, their elbows on the table, grinning.

"Love?", Orchid asked in a soft and inquisitive tone.

Gwen looked up, smiled and sighed, slightly pushing her body away from the table with her hands. "I remember my first boyfriend", she started. "He was so gentle at first, he treated me with respect… He was never late, he always paid attention to me, like if I was a very important part of his life… Maybe the most important part…"

She kept on looking up with a smile, apparently dreaming of the past, her eyes gazing towards something immaterial. "But…"

"He was too immature… I guess it's normal for boys his age. We kept on being friends, and I tried to have what I had with him with other guys, but…" She sighed again, this time losing her smile, still dreaming of the past. "The most important thing about a guy… Is that he makes you feel… like you're the most important part of his life. As if he just couldn't live without you."

She looked at Orchid, who was letting Gwen's words penetrate her soul, listening attentively, paying absolutely no attention to any other noise occurring around her. "You know you're in love when you guys have that. And then he protects you, and makes you feel safe. And you like being with him, no matter what you guys do, and he likes being with you too, and there's nothing he would rather do than be with you", Gwen went on.

Orchid thought about her relationship with Yusuke, and indeed knew that she liked being with him, that he made her feel safe, and that, at times, there was nothing she would rather do than be with him. Maybe then, she was in love?

Hitomi looked at Orchid with all the seriousness in the world. "Have you guys ever kissed?", she asked. "Kissed?", Orchid replied with a her soft tone, blushing. The two other girls waited patiently and silently for an answer that just wasn't coming. Gwen just went ahead and assumed.

"You two will get closer together… And then, your gazes will converge, and the rest will flow naturally, by itself. And if he's the right one for you, your heart will pound, you will melt in his arms, you will feel like the fabric of time stopped moving expressly for the two of you, and you will feel like you were his for the taking."

The three girls paused a long time to reflect on Gwen's words, the vapour of their hot chocolate rising up and filling the air around them.

* * *

Gwen looked at her father cultivate the lands near her wooden house, as she sat down on the porch, legs crossed and swinging in the air. She was enjoying the tranquil breeze that was blowing over the countryside house, smiling, her eyes closed, listening to the sounds of her strong father as he worked. She enjoyed the smell of fresh green grass, mixed with the smell of the soup that her mother was preparing for dinner.

Suddenly, she felt something furry rub itself against her hand, and opened her eyes to see her cat. She grinned upon seeing the animal, and grabbed it with her two hands, bringing its face close to hers.

"Hello, you!" The cat mewed in satisfaction as she stroked its light brown fur with her hands. "How are you?" The little cat swung its limbs in the air. She gently allowed the cat to rest on her knees, and continued to stroke its fur. Her father had stopped working the fields,and had approached her.

"Your mother says dinner is ready", the father told Gwen, speaking in Welsh English. "We'll be waiting for you inside."

"Sure 'pa", she replied in her native tongue, and she continued to stroke her cat's fur as her father went in the house. The blue-grey sky became grey, suggesting, along with the humidity, that rain was going to fall soon.

She noticed a boy was looking at her, standing up on the fields. He was dressed in corduroy pants, a shirt and a small vest. He looked at her, seriously, and she looked back at him, puzzled. Her mouth was opened, as if to speak, but no sound would come out. Seconds later, the boy was sitting next to her on the wooden porch, legs swinging in the air, hands on his knees. Both looked to the ground, avoiding eye contact.

"Am I… ever going to see you again?", the boy asked, breaking the silence.

Gwen lowered her gaze even more, very timid. "Thomas, don't say things like that…"

"But you're going to Japan… Are you ever coming back?", the boy asked, one more time.

Gwen maintained her gaze fixed to the ground. "No", she said, with more maturity than one would give credit for an eleven year old girl. The boy was obviously shaken by that answer,but did not speak. They both kept staring at their feet and didn't say a word. After a moment's silence, she changed her mind. "Maybe."

Another silence.

"Yes." Gwen looked at her friend with seriousness, then a smile. "Yes", she finally said, with more assurance, then she looked back again, to the ground, avoiding any possible eye contact. A few drops pounded on her white blouse. It started raining, but neither of them wanted to move, not from that porch, not from each other.

* * *

Orchid was sitting on a small wooden bridge, her legs dangling in the air, rocking back and forth alternatively. She held a fishing rod in her hands and was patiently waiting to catch something. Anything. Her father was sitting besides her, also holding a fishing rod. They were both patiently sitting and waiting, silent. She looked at him with a smile, and fondness. He reciprocated the smile.

This was truly a magical moment for her. The sky was red as the sun was setting, and she was spending time with the one person that meant everything to her. Suddenly, something seemed to grab her fishing rod. She turned her attention away form her father, and to the water. He put his fishing rod away, stood up and knelt down behind his daughter, holding her hands with his, helping her complete that catch. They tried mightily, but the creature got away. Orchid moaned in disappointment, but her father reassured her, there were plenty more to be caught.

* * *

"You want me to read your future?", Hitomi asked Orchid, pulling her out of her reverie. She held a pack of tarot cards in her hands.

Gwen looked at her with little, dubious eyes. "Hitomi, those things are for the superstitious only…"

"Not true!", Hitomi replied with fervor, "we in the School of Mysticism can be taught to understand and read the odds, so they can be revealed to us when we want to know, and these cards are special tarot cards! I can really read the future with these cards!"

Orchid was enthusiastic, and looked at Hitomi with eyes big with excitement. "Really?"

"Yep, I'll just take a few cards out of this pack right here…", Hitomi said. A pinkish glow surrounded her body for a few moments. She shuffled the pack and pulled five cards out of it, at random, after having closed her eyes and focused. She quickly displayed the cards in front of her, and without reading, put the first one she had drawn on the table. On it was the symbol of a woman of breathtaking beauty, a succubus, whose black wings were similar to those of a bat, and whose skin was of a pinkish hue, held in the arms of a majestic man clad in iron armor. Hitomi's face reveled upon seeing the card.

"See? This card is the first one I draw, and reveals a not so distant future; one could even say it is the present. It is entitled the love of Rose and Raiden; it means that you'll meet someone that will be very special to you, and you two will fall in deep love, even if that love could be a little wild and dangerous…"

Orchid looked at the card with sparkling eyes, and waited impatiently to hear more. Hitomi put the second card on the table; it was that of a knight clad in iron armor, and a green dragon appearing behind this man. Hitomi's smile did not wither.

"This card is the second I pulled out, and is a little more distant into the future, but not so much. It is entitled "Dragoneer"; it means that your lover will protect you to the bitter hand!"

Orchid was too enthusiastic to speak, and Gwen started to pay a bit more attention, visibly interested. Hitomi was about to draw the third card, but stopped and looked at it first. She saw a black card on which were illustrated human skulls lying on a deserted pathway. Her smile withered. The signification of the card was clear: “Death and suffering”. She was not about to reveal this to Orchid.

She looked at the other cards. The second one had the picture of two bare chested women standing up, one in front of the other, as if they were antagonists. One had skin of a reddish hue, while the other had skin of a blueish hue. They held their hands upward, to the sky. This card she wasn’t sure if she wanted to reveal to Orchid, nor did she know about its signification. The card was entitled, “Clash of the goddesses”.

Both Gwen and Orchid waited impatiently for the other cards to be revealed. Orchid’s eyes were still sparkling with excitement. Hitomi looked at the final card and saw nothing but the color black on it. This card is the equivalent of a joker in any normal pack of cards, its signification is unknown to all. The card is entitled “Unknown”, and its signification, as she picked it up last, is simply that Orchid’s distant future cannot be read.

Hitomi looked at her two friends, who were patiently waiting for the rest of the forecast, put back the cards in her pack of cards, and shuffled it. Her friends looked at her with incomprehension before she muttered these words: “We’ll be late.”

* * *

Orchid took off her mitts and put them in her locker, then did the same for her pink coat. She ran a hand through her hair, wet by the snowflakes that had fallen on it and melted. She closed her locker, and walked the stairs up to the school's hallway. She noticed there was a lot of noise, and many students were gathered in front of a wall, whispering.

When she approached that wall, some of them were looking at her, with some curiosity. She wondered what was going on, so she frayed herself a little way through the crowd and saw papers on the wall. She understood, as she read those papers, why everyone was excited: those were the results of the first midterm exams, categorized per student and per class. She also understood why some people were looking at her with curiosity: she, Orchid Tanaka, got the best scores, and ranked first in all her midterms so far. Claire Wright ranked second, and Bleu Heisashi, third. Gwen joined up behind her and whistled, impressed.

"Keep it up, genius!", she said. Orchid looked back at her with a smile, encouraged. "You're new here, and I don't want to spoil the surprise", Gwen continued, "but if you do well like that for the finals, something good happens!", with her usual huge grin. "Not putting pressure on you or anything, of course."

Orchid looked at Gwen with excitement, wondering what kind of compelling secret her friend was hiding from her. She could wait.

* * *

Hitomi, Orchid and Gwen lied on the white snow that covered the ground, in a field near school. They were lying on their backs, feet outward, their hair brushing against that of the other, in a circle. One had her mitts pressed against the ground,while the other had their mitts pressed against their chest. They looked up to the night sky, and contemplated the bright stars. Only the noise of an occasional car passing by disturbed the tranquillity of this moment.

Small white fog came out of Orchid's mouth as she breathed through the cold air. She looked at the stars, eyes sparkling, reveling.

"In the school of mysticism", Hitomi started, "we learn the meaning of constellations of stars, and the exact moments and locations where we can see them best. We can learn to harness them in order to cast certain spells."

Orchid was listening, attentive to Hitomi's words.

Hitomi pointed up to a succession of stars with her mitt, and in this manner, drew something resembling a hunter. "This one is the constellation of Orion", she said. Then, she pointed to another succession of stars and drew something resembling a lion. "This one is the constellation of Leo", she said. She pointed to another succession of stars, and drew something resembling a scorpion. "And this is the constellation of the Scorpius".

She went on, drawing with her hand and pointing to stars, enumerating all the constellations she could possibly discern in the black night sky. And Orchid kept on listening, fascinated like a child. After some time, the three girls lied on the ground, quiet, their chests moving up and down as they breathed, reflecting on the magnificence of the astral bodies.

After some time, a shooting star cut through the sky, and caught their attention. Orchid drew one breath of marvel.

"It's…", she started. Gwen interrupted her. "Shush."

They waited for the shooting star to finish its slow course through the sky. It was Gwen who then initiated a conversation.

"So what did you wish for?", Gwen asked. Orchid looked at her with an inquisitive look. "Wish?", Orchid asked. "It is a myth that shooting stars are related to good fortune. Besides, what have you got to lose?"

Orchid looked up again, quiet, and paused.

Then she closed her eyes, and wished for something in her heart.

* * *

Upon returning home, she closed the entrance door behind her, and awkwardly got rid of her small leather ankle-boots with her feet. She then awkwardly removed her mitts and put them on the sofa near the entrance, then zipped down her pink winter coat, removed it from her soft body, and also put it on the same sofa.

She tiptoed her way through the dark, careful not to make the slightest noise with her soft, white cotton socks as she gently put one set of toes in front of the other, feeling the wall on her side with her hand to maintain her balance and sense of direction where her sight couldn't pierce through the shadows, advancing through the unlit hallway towards a room where light transpired.

When she arrived in front of the room, she saw Yusuke, standing up, removing his shirt with the intention of putting on his pajamas. She saw the details of the muscles that composed his athletic body, on his arms, and his back. For a minute, it seemed like the world had stopped moving, just for her, for them both. Time stopped, and it was only the two of them. Her heart pounded, her breasts quivered, her lips trembled.

She remained standing there, looking at him, speechless.

And he remained standing there, looking at her, speechless.

Fact sheet: Gwen Savage

Characteristics:
Academic specialization: Orchid School of Magic, school of Regeneration
Date of birth: 27th of September 2003
Blood type: AB
Hair style: Long shiny blond hair
Height: 150 lbs
Weight: 5′5 ft

About Gwen Savage:

Gwen Savage was born in Wales in a relatively poor family of Welsh-speaking farmers and agriculture workers of Anglican Protestant faith, although her family's talent as magical healers, acquired empirically rather than through formal education,helped in the healthy growth of their harvest.

Through the financial assistance of the British government for students wishing to study abroad, through assistance from her uncle and aunt, and thanks to money she earns working part-time at a coffee shop in Tokyo, she manages to study in the Japanese Orchid School of Magic and acquire the best of educations. She is also furthering her knowledge of her family's magical talents.

To study in Japan, she left her mother, her father and her childhood sweetheart Thomas Mulligan, although she will be returning to the United Kingdom once her high school studies are over. She is currently a 12th grader, and is in her last year of studies in high school. Upon completion of this academic year, she plans to undertake University studies in the field of either nursing, or if she is lucky enough to have the appropriate grades, medicine.

She is very protective, and acts like a big sister to Orchid (or, as she calls the red-haired maiden, Orchy). She enjoys going to coffee shops, talking, going to the mall and also enjoys other outdoor activities. Along with Hitomi, she had a few friends of her own before the arrival of Orchid, but this year, she has concentrated her attention and affection more onto Orchid and Hitomi, with whom she feels a deeper connection.

Gary Germeil

House

I had nowhere to go when I was released from detox, so I started bumming around NA meetings and got hooked up with a room in a, co-ed halfway house near the train station. I was on-again, off-again at this point. Mostly on-again.

It was only a ten-minute walk to Central Carolina's campus, where I met up with Bill and Haley. They'd fronted all the money. I could have ran with it, maybe I should have, but on my way over, when the sky turned purple and the dead light on the edge of town washed away the stars, I suddenly needed company. We wanted a roof and somewhere out of the way to sit and get high without judgment. I knew of the house from way back. It'd been abandoned since before I went to jail.

Rural Route 404 took us just beyond the city limits. Grime streaked the windshield in half crescents, but the car was nice and still smelled new. Haley sat up front with Bill. Alone in the back seat, I prodded the open window with my cigarette. When we found the house, Bill pulled right up on the lawn and parked around back. Fried grass and dandelions slumped beneath an old tire swing hanging from a single, crooked tree. We walked around a burned out fire pit full of grey charcoal and bones. The moon stood oblonged and contorted in the sky.

"I've heard things about this place," Bill said.

It was a mansion, strung up with tattered yellow tape. The back porch smiled.

"No one's gonna bother us," I said. I pushed the tire swing and watched it spin without really seeing it. "We can go back to your dorm if you want."

"I think it's exciting." Haley said, running past us both. Her faded white dress brushed a bald spot on the lawn and kicked up dust as she skipped ahead.

"I'm not going in," Bill said.

"C'mon, sweetie," she said, and walked backwards up the steps.

I followed her towards the door.

A light went on behind a second story window.

"You see that?" Bill pointed.

Haley and I looked up our necks exposed, almost parallel to the ground. I could barely make out a blotted figure behind the window.

"Let's find out who it is," Haley said.

"They probably just want to be left alone," I said. "Maybe we'll make some new friends." I ducked under the yellow police tape and opened the door; Haley followed. The smell of cold sweat and fever moved past us towards Bill who steadied himself against the frame. A cloud of mothballs and rot hung in the room.

The torn carpet buoyed bottles and cans, cooked tin foil and broken glass lay tucked into corners. Music played in another room. Fucking, Bob Seger.

"We're cool," I said.

Haley cleaned a spot around an old table by the staircase, happily arranging three mismatched chairs, and used a ratty oven mitt to push an empty picture frame and a pile of cigarette butts into an empty case of beer.

Bill stayed by the door.

"What a spot," Haley said.

"In or out, man," I asked Bill.

He just stood there watching Haley rearrange the living room.

A door slammed above the ceiling, and a noise stumbled down the stairs. A face appeared, a young girl no more than 15 in a faded white dress carrying a jug of wine looking like a corpse. She stared at me as she steadied herself, and the rings below our eyes danced together while my sight adjusted. Bill ran after her when she flew past him out the door.

I spent the long night wound up in a ball of teeth

chattering conversation with Haley, thinking about the ghost and what it would be like to sit in the empty space haunted by the frayed hem of her dress and all the things that would never be the same after that night.

Afternoon edged into evening when we woke up curled up under a pile of old curtains, soaked in sweat and smelling of dust. We lost a whole day's worth of sun. Fairly certain it was a Thursday, we set out for Wild Flowers to find Bill and his car. If we were right, he'd be sitting in the back room full of TV's and newspaper clippings with Tom, taking bets on the weekend's high school football games. I hung out at the bar with him and Haley most days, before we went to meetings to get our slips signed.

I started using the waist strap of my backpack; I wrapped it around me in case anyone got any ideas of ripping me off. I listened to my never-ending supply of pills shake as we humped along the side of the country road. The stuff was easy enough to move; I sold a lot, but I never seemed to have any money.

"It's so empty out here," Haley said. Her hair was dull and stiff like straw.

"It's nice," I said, and it was. The evening was one of those perfect ones you get in the late summer where you're actually glad you slept all day. It was unseasonably cool, the first bite of autumn.

I patted myself down. Keys, meeting list, pocket-sized note book, a couple grams of pot, pack of cigarettes (seven cigs and the better part of a joint), wallet (sixteen bucks, unused Durham Bulls ticket, flyer for an after-hours club, Zig Zags).

We chased the horizon west and watched the town's modest skyline crest in front of us. "I miss my dog," Haley said.

"Me too," I said, even though I didn't have a dog. We

smoked the rest of the joint and watched the clouds turn pink and darken as our hands steadied and our thoughts slowed.

"You think about getting clean ever?" she asked.

"All the time," I said.

"I don't think Bill is coming back," she said.

"How?" I asked.

"He's never left me somewhere," she said.

Haley and I didn't touch each other last night. I had enough on my mind without pissing off Bill, plus she has track marks and kids. Her blue eyes look dark, a patch of freckles bridging her nose. She is pretty, but spaced out: Like she used to be really smart and sometimes she realizes it, and it pisses her off that she can't put things together the way she seems to know she should. I understood.

"Who knows," I said. A speeding pick-up followed by a cop car flew past us and turned into a cloud of dust near the bridge into town.

"This is it for me," she said.

"What?"

"I had a friend," she said. "We shot up in my car, and she turned blue. It's amazing how quickly you turn blue when you stop breathing." Haley closed her eyes for a second, and I thought she might trip over something. "I drove as fast as I could, across town to the good part of the city. I thought I left her outside of the ER, but it was an office building. It hit me when I was about halfway home. I never tried to find out what happened."

"Jesus," I said.

"She looked just like that fucking girl last night," she said, "I couldn't figure out who she reminded me of until just now."

Her blue eyes looked tired and dark, but spoke of greater things. It's the only time I'd ever seen someone have this kind of realization and I resented her for it. As if there

was one moment up for grabs between the two of us and it slipped through my hands – like I was grabbing fucking air.
"Did she die?" I asked.
"It was a long time ago," she said.
We walked in silence for a while, twitching at the sound of our own footsteps.
"I'm gonna go to the clinic," she said. "Get on Methadone. I can go to technical school, or maybe study to be a vet tech. I could take care of puppies."
"Admitting you're powerless is the first step," I said, but what did I know?
I waited for her to say just one more night and for me to say yes. For us to turn back and go to the house under the guise of summoning the spirit of her friend or something and then Haley would end up killing herself somehow; she'd OD, or maybe fall down the stairs and break her neck, or just walk out into traffic like she was following some vision of her daughter or her friend or dog, just fucking vanish like Billy. But she didn't.
We got back into town just as the street-lights flickered to life. Her hair sang like fire as we passed in and out of the shadows on the sidewalk. When we stopped in front of Wild Flowers, she got on her tip-toes and kissed me on the cheek. It felt warm. She said goodbye and kept walking.

Ben Gwin

The Flap of a Butterfly's Wings…

Katrina was her name when she hit
Knocked down walls, lives, more than a bit
With time-machine of wonder, so geophysical
I announced to the world, I would distill
Source, roots of her being, so terrible

Rizzle, bizzle, hoot, toot-sizzle and I was
Off overseas tracing a time-stormy past
Ravaging nature, Atlantic's broad back
Reversing time, storm's inclinations, Bahamas
Time's backward magic, decelerating dramas

Tropical Depression 12, August 23 2005
T'was more or less as I say, describe
Current flow, from African air asunder
Sahara, ominous, thunderous –zaaapppps!
Frightened butterfly, days before, wings' flaps…

Beautiful delicate wings, gold, azure
Was Katrina's source, I'll assure
Butterfly, egg, cocoon, caterpillar past
To world, turbulence forever cast
Minor movements, consequences vast

Minute vibrations, atmospheres recast
From place, tranquil beauty unsurpassed
Removed from Jazz, Mardi Gras, shrimp repast
Bourbon Street, stately homes, Superdome
Levee break, lives at stake, political palindrome:

Are we not drawn onward, we few, drawn onward to a new era?
Helicopter wings, Marine One, beings weak, Brownie's chimera?
Flooded horrors front photo ops, city's time, trade, dead

stop
Forward machine of time, city awash, slime, crime, partisan slop
HELP US, rescue sign read, black people implored on that one rooftop!

max keanu

Margaret
It is New Year's Day,
1852, the same year
I am going to die.
I don't know that yet.
My future husband fidgets
under his freshly starched
collar. He will leave me here
in the ground come September,
head out west to California
with his two brothers

chasing the gold
of sunsets. Who knows,
maybe he finds some.
The brothers will die
en route, one of Typhus,
the other robbed, beaten,
and stabbed. I won't know
any of this. I'll only know
how lovely I look in mother's
chiffon and lace, my barely
more than a girl blue
saucer eyes veiled

to what awaits
on my wedding night
and further on. I am light
as the sifting snow swirls
through the churchyard
graveyard. The same
I will lie in later
this autumn,

in this same snow
white gown, dreaming
my perfect children softly
playing in the late afternoon
half-light before my dream
house, Nathaniel slanting
slowly across the sun
burnt field, his golden
arms laden
with plenty.

brion berkshire

Returning Home During Rutting Season

In the dark before dawn the bucks are out
and moving. ,*Probably sniffing out the good pussy,*
I laugh, pleased with myself for a moment.
Caught in the glare of the headlight, one stands
as if confused, embarrassed as if I had caught him
about to do something he might be ashamed of.
Go ahead, I say. Get yours. Follow your need.

And I know he will get his
alright. Somewhere in the early dapple
of gray, amongst the dwarf pine smell and
the sweet camphor of other, he'll find it,
the what he is missing, and lose all sense
of decorum and mount her regardless of his
awkwardness, all muscle and pulsing belief
that this is exactly what he should be doing,
flinging forward until he is truly grace-full,
and the ache comes out of him through
the dark sepulcher of his throat and into
his grave mouth with such animal force
as to nearly tear his straining face off,
the groan-sound so completely frightening
and familiar to every familial creature
within hearing, or even without, that
they will pause for a moment and feel
his wild abandonment, or fear.

I will be back home by then, snuggled
beneath the warmth of thick blankets
waiting for morning. And I'll say a little
prayer for him who has no need for prayer,
nor god nor towered cathedral, but lives
according to his true nature, pray that
the hunters in the trees are slow and

their sites are somehow off today,
or their guns jam, or they've fallen
asleep; that there be some grace
left somewhere that will allow
this one living thing
to find its secret, terrible bliss
in this vast, unraveling world.

brion Berkshire

Kids

The thin pieces of copper lay on the hard pumice filled
rocks
Waiting for us to find them; Pennies
We were kids doing whatever we could to get the
boredom to end in the little town we lived in.
Pigeons were a good past time, we killed them as
sharpshooters with our scopes and daisy bb guns-
We would plink them off the thin wires with glass tops
that looked like bells of crystal, some were green but they
all shattered when you shot at them.
Fossils, look I found one, walking the tracks that lead to
nowhere we found then in the heated days
Crime was something other towns had, we were
protected…
Thanks Dad!

Greg Lyvers

It

It shook me to the core.
This was the first time I knew that real evil existed.
I was quiet and I sat there like a child on the brink of
crying,
in those moments that you do not know what to think.
I felt it.
It came near me and sickness filled my stomach like bad
water
from a garden hose. My thoughts were to cry out to God ,
to
scream in terror but I couldn't.
It touched me.
It laid over me like a cold, wet, towel covering my shell.
I only knew I needed to escape. Everything in that
moment
told me to run but I remained petrified and unable to
move.
It spoke to me.
My heart sank, I felt like I was going to pass out then in
an
instant;
It was gone.
Leaving me with my sour stomach and the hair raised on
the
back of my neck.
Finally my flesh let loose a sigh,
I wept.

Greg Lyvers

Previously printed in "Snips of Time" (Lulu.com)

7263707R0

Made in the USA
Charleston, SC
10 February 2011